A SURVIVAL KIT FOR WIVES

A SURVIVAL KIT FOR WIVES

HOW TO AVOID FINANCIAL CHAOS BEFORE TRAGEDY STRIKES

by
Don & Renee Martin
with
Joan Scobey,
editor

VILLARD BOOKS   **NEW YORK 1986**

Library of Congress Cataloging in Publication Data

Martin, Don, 1937–
  A survival kit for wives.

  1. Wives—Finance, Personal. 2. Widows—Finance,
Personal. I. Martin, Renee. II. Scobey, Joan.
III. Title.
HG179.M3427 1986   332.024′0655   85–40182
ISBN 0–394–74361–X

Manufactured in United States of America

9 8 7 6 5 4 3 2

This book
is
lovingly
dedicated
to our
daughters,

Michelle, Jennifer, and Samantha

ACKNOWLEDGMENTS

Our very special thanks to all the women who openly shared their personal experiences with us. Not only do they add a human impact to the book, but their examples motivated us to speed our work on this project.

- Joan Scobey, more than just our editor, who contributed immensely with her excellent ability at organization, constant probing questions, and professional skill and attitude.
- Shelli Chosak, M.A., psychologist and family therapist, for her counsel, guidance, and encouragement. She was available throughout the last two years to offer her expertise, thoughts, and opinions.
- Ida Fisher, co-author of *The Widow's Guide to Life,* a wonderful resource and inspiration for women who want to be self-reliant. We are grateful for the hours of wisdom she shared with us.
- Mary Keller, vice president of human resources with Wherehouse Entertainment, Inc., for her valuable suggestions for women seeking employment.
- Wayne Casey, attorney, Reish and Davis, for helping us translate the complexities of estate planning into basic English.
- Susan Gilmour, M.L.S., who researched and compiled the Sources of Information.
- Mary Whittaker, attorney, of Lewis, D'Amato, Brisbois and Bisgaard, for her legal expertise on wills and guardians.
- Teri Wilde, corporate banking officer with Bank of America, for her knowledge of banking institutions.
- Ron D. Makela, vice president, Santa Monica Bank, for arranging interviews with his very professional banking officers, and participating in the many meetings we had.

● Kathleen Ethridge, trust department officer, Santa Monica Bank, for clarifying the functions and benefits of trust departments.
● Pat Young-Spivak, loan officer, Santa Monica Bank, for her excellent explanations of borrowing from financial institutions.

Our special thanks to many people in the Cal-Surance Group, specifically:

● Lennie Faragallah, ChFC, CLU, who assisted with technical advice about life insurance.
● Nancy Collinge, CPCU, CPIW, for information about car insurance.
● Mary Shelton, AIM, CPIW, who critiqued the insurance chapters.

And to:

● Maryann Rimoin, who assisted in proofreading and coordinating the manuscript.
● Leslie Rodriguez, who typed, and typed, and typed!
● Vivian Dondero, our liaison and coordinator with Villard Books.

We are also indebted to many other people for their valuable comments and contributions to various parts of the manuscript.

CONTENTS

WORKSHEETS, CHECKLISTS, AND INFORMATION SHEETS

Numbered sheets and lists to be filled in are in the Workbook section; information sheets are within the relevant chapters.

1 KEEPING FAMILY RECORDS AND DOCUMENTS

16 WHEN A DEATH OCCURS

18 THE JOB MARKET

INTRODUCTION

Can you answer these questions:

- What are your assets? How much are they worth?
- Do you know how to get a loan? Could you qualify for one?
- Who has access to your safe-deposit box? Where is the key?
- Will your children have money for college if your family income drops?
- How do you get emergency cash if your husband is out of town or becomes ill?
- Will your medical insurance cover a long-term illness?
- How much life insurance does your husband have? Where are the policies?
- Where is your husband's will? What does it say?

If you answered "no" or "I don't know" to any of these you're in good company. Most women (and a lot of men) are woefully disorganized about vital family information. We know where the safe-deposit box is, but we've lost track of the key—or who can use it. We pay life insurance premiums, but we don't know what the policies are currently worth—or if they still cover us adequately. We have medical insurance, but we don't know if it includes a long-term disability. We don't even know how much we're worth. Most of us know just enough to lull us into a false sense of security, and security—your family's security—is precisely what is at risk.

Most of us muddle along until something jolts us into action. In our case, it was a car accident. We weren't in it, thank goodness, but it shattered the lives of two of our good friends. John was killed outright, and Betty was so badly injured she was hospitalized for almost a year. We're not sure when—or if—she'll recover completely.

Their tragic accident shocked us—and it unnerved us. What if that had happened to us? Who would take care of our children? Would our friends even know whom to notify? We took long hard looks at our family arrangements. We thought we were pretty savvy about them, but there were still loose ends we hadn't considered. The most important was that our children wouldn't have adequate information about our family's household business. From that terrible accident we were learning some valuable lessons, the hard way.

As we tried to help Betty, we found ourselves making lists, getting information for her lawyer, her doctors, her insurance broker. We began to see just what you'd need to get your family's business in order, in this or any other emergency. Our lists turned into worksheets, and the information into guidelines; we put them all away for our own future reference. By this time we were working at least as hard for our own protection as for Betty's.

One evening at dinner we met a woman who had been widowed a few years ago. We told her about our project.

"Oh, how I wish I'd had a workbook like that before my husband died," she said. "What trouble it would have saved me with probate, Rob's business partners, just everything. Our affairs were a mess!"

And that's how we started *A Survival Kit for Wives*.

You'll notice we're talking about wives. We want to talk to you and your husband while you can still plan to avoid common financial pitfalls, while your best friend and most trusted advisor—your husband—is still around to help you.

Most women aren't prepared for the event they fear most: the death or illness of their husbands. Even a psychologist we interviewed, who readily understands the process of denial in her patients, ironically couldn't help herself. "When Arnie first got sick, we didn't want to talk about it," she told us. "We were afraid that if we put his affairs in order, then it would really happen."

Other women were terrifyingly ignorant about their economic status. "For five years after my husband died, I had no idea of my financial situation," a California widow told us. "I was living in limbo until the estate was settled."

Women (and men) who do have resources often lack the skills and financial knowledge to ensure their long-term economic survival. "My husband left me $300,000 in insurance, and I didn't have the faintest idea what to do with it," said a schoolteacher. "What's worse, I was besieged with conflicting advice."

Among the women we interviewed, the most common and painful reaction was the paralyzing inability to make important decisions when they were first engulfed by the trauma of widowhood or divorce, or burdened by a seriously ill or disabled husband. "For months after Mark died, I didn't know whether to sell the house or not," says a Texas journalist. "I couldn't even decide whether to sell his car or mine."

As we talked to more and more widows and divorcées, we began to get an important message. As unsettling as it may have been for these women to talk about death and divorce, they claimed it was more terrifying not to be prepared for them. "Don't wait till it happens!" women told us urgently, time after time.

We also discovered that when you get your family's business in order, and know how to handle difficult situations when they arise, some splendid things can happen—for both men and women. Universally, wives feel a wonderful sense of self-sufficiency, independence, strength, and competence, all within a loving interdependent relationship. Grateful husbands experience comfort and relief when their wives understand family business and can independently cope with crises, large and small.

The promise of *A Survival Kit for Wives* is peace of mind. For women we offer an emotional life raft of knowledge and preparation that will see them through any crisis; for men, the reassurance that comes from safeguarding their legacy and preventing a future financial disaster.

A Survival Kit for Wives will help you organize all your family's essential information sensibly and efficiently. Its unique format is your tailor-made kit for economic survival. The text is a reference library of expert advice on the financial, legal, and practical realities of taking care of the business of your family. The Workbook section at the end of the book becomes a permanent archive of your essential family information—just as soon as you fill it in. This detachable section has clear, simple worksheets on which to record all the indispensable information about your family's most important papers and private business, checklists to remind you of what to do in an emergency, and information sheets to help you do it.

Using the Worksheets

Most of us respect books too much to write in them. That's why *A Survival Kit for Wives* is in the form of a workbook. We invite you to write in it. We beg you to write in it. The best way to honor the intent of *A Survival Kit for Wives* is to make notes on its pages, underline its text, make computations in the margins. And especially, fill in the worksheets and checklists. Use it.

This book is designed to be easy to use. You'll find all the worksheets in the last section of the book. Each one is titled, numbered, and cross-referenced to its explanatory text so you can flip back and forth between the body of the book and the worksheets.

The entire Workbook section is perforated so you can store it in your safe-deposit box, duplicate it for other members of your family or your advisors, or just take certain worksheets with you when you meet with your advisors. It also allows you to complete the forms while they're still in the book, or detach them first if that's easier for you.

As you read the text, you'll note that some information should be updated periodically. This means you'll need additional copies of those worksheets for the future. There are also circumstances—for example, if you have two houses, or two cars—when you'll need multiple copies right away. Before you use any worksheet, duplicate it so you'll always have at least one blank copy in reserve—do it right from the book, or detach the page first.

Getting Started

The hardest thing about getting started is . . . getting started. If preparing for a tragedy before it happens puts you off, consider instead the happier benefits of having your family records in order. That's what occurred to our friend Dorothy, who wants to open a retail shop. "As soon as I fill out the worksheets on my assets and net worth," she said gleefully, "I bet the bank will talk to me more seriously about a loan."

Most women won't have the information to complete a net worth statement—or a lot of other family records, either—on their own. You'll need help from your husband. Some men will be receptive and responsive to your request, others will resist sharing financial and legal records. And that's understandable. This is a topic that can be uncomfortable.

We know many husbands who've said, "Well, you know my accountant knows everything, my attorney knows everything, just talk to them if anything happens."

One wife replied, "I realize that your attorney and your accountant know everything, but I feel so insecure. I'd really feel a lot better if I understood enough to know what questions to ask them."

Another told her reluctant husband, "I wouldn't want my ignorance to destroy what you've built up. One way of avoiding that is to learn a little more about what's going on, so I can protect your interests."

A third wife, who felt strongly about being responsible for herself as a woman, simply said to her husband, "I'd like to learn more about the financial affairs of our household. I just realized I want to take more responsibility in our partnership." He was surprised by the depth of her commitment, she reported, and pleased. "I felt a little like Eliza Dolittle triumphantly becoming a 'consort battleship' to Henry Higgins."

Use *A Survival Kit for Wives* at your own pace, to meet your own current needs. Don't expect, or even try, to complete all the worksheets in a short period of time. We do suggest, however, that you begin with the first chapter, Keeping Family Records and Documents. Those worksheets are easily completed, and you'll be glad to have that information immediately. Then complete the chapters that are most important to you. You may want to get right to the analysis of your health insurance in Chapters 12 and 13, Serious Illness and Disability, for example, and leave Chapter 3, Figuring Your Net Worth, for last. Or jump straight to the last chapter, The Job Market, and leave Borrowing, Chapter 5, for a rainy day.

The next time you're quizzed on your family's business, you'll have all the answers. You provided them.

I

BASIC
SURVIVAL
SAVVY

KEEPING FAMILY RECORDS AND DOCUMENTS

1

Some people keep them in shoe boxes, some people file them neatly in folders, and a lot of people stuff them into desk drawers. Everybody has a different way of dealing with family records, but what they all have in common is the desperate hope that when they need an important document, they can find it.

Sometimes you're lucky, but luck is a pretty slim reed to lean on when you're talking about your family's most important papers.

We have a neighbor who runs mostly on luck. It usually holds out—but not always. Every year before he goes off on vacation, he makes his Annual Passport Search. One year he found it in his golf bag (he'd been golfing in Scotland the previous summer), and one year he found it with his camera gear. Last year he couldn't find it for days, and even laid-back Tom was beginning to get a little frantic. But at the last minute it turned up—in his desk drawer. When he opened it, he saw that it had expired two months earlier.

Being organized, however, doesn't carry any guarantee, as Kathy, a young Kansas teacher, found out to her dismay. Kathy is married to a man who likes to handle all the family business on his own. Dan pays the bills and keeps track of the family papers. Kathy never thought about the ar-rangement—until Dan had a heart attack.

"It was a mess," said Kathy as she recalled the first days of her husband's illness. "Dan was in intensive care and I had to get into the safe-deposit box. Dan's secretary finally found the key, but the bank wouldn't let me open the box. They said I didn't have legal access to it."

Dan prided himself on his organization, but he was the only one who knew where everything was. Thinking he was safeguarding their important documents, for example, Dan kept them neatly in the safe-deposit box. "He never realized that no one else in the family knew where the key was, and couldn't use it anyway," said Kathy.

This time, Dan and Kathy were lucky. Although Dan was hooked up to heart-monitoring equipment, he could still sign his name on the bank's signature card and give other people access to the safe-deposit box.

Sam is a dentist we know who also keeps his records carefully filed. When the Internal Revenue Service notified him of an audit, Sam said, "My heart started to pound, but at least I didn't have the added anxiety of wondering where my records were." All his canceled checks and receipts were neatly filed, going back the requisite seven years.

Most people aren't as organized as Sam and Dan. They have important papers scattered all over—in bureau drawers at home, in office files, at a lawyer's, at a parent's house—and, like our neighbor, all too often they don't remember where the different documents are. Not only are these people disorganized, but they have put irreplaceable records in jeopardy.

The problem with important papers is you never know when you'll need them. Your family documents are required for any number of reasons that would never occur to you. After you get married, for instance, you have to produce your birth certificate in order to change your driver's license to your married name. When our daughter Samantha was eight and proudly opened her first bank account, she was surprised to learn she had to supply her Social Security number, along with her hard-earned savings.

Every family needs a system of maintaining records. Whether you're going overseas and need your passport, receive an unwelcome query from the Internal Revenue Service about a previous tax return, are moving to a new house, or selling a stock, you want to be able to put your hands on a document when you need it. What's more, we know you don't want to drown in paper; you want to keep just what you need, for as long as you need it, and no longer.

That's why we've worked out a detailed explanation of what important documents and records you should keep, where you should keep them, and for how long. Then we keyed this information to a series of worksheets on which to record this information for your family. As you'll see, together they give you a foolproof system for keeping records. The worksheets alone form a summary of your family's business that you'll find useful in many circumstances, and invaluable in an emergency.

YOUR IMPORTANT PAPERS AND WHERE TO KEEP THEM

There are many documents you should keep permanently, but there are others you only need for short periods. Some are safest in a bank vault. Others should never be kept in a safe-deposit box, in case it's sealed at the time of a death. In this chapter you'll learn where and how long to safeguard your documents.

You can keep your papers in a variety of places: a home file, in the office, or with your attorney, accountant, financial planner, tax consultant, or other close advisor. If records are difficult to replace, keep them in a safe-deposit box or in a fire-resistant container at home. Use only an insulated steel box that is labeled "fire resistant" and guaranteed to protect the contents against fire for at least one hour.

If we don't suggest a place to keep a particular document, you can keep it anywhere—just be sure other family members and/or friends know where that is. The best way to keep them informed is to give each a copy of the first worksheet, *Location of Important Papers*, which lists all your family documents and where they can be found.

Personal Documents

Certificates of birth.   If you don't have birth certificates for every member of your family, take the time to get them now. They're needed for many things, from passport applications to the completion of death certificates.

For a nominal fee you can obtain copies of birth certificates in person or by mail from the County Hall of Records where the individual was born.

Be sure each copy is certified, that is, stamped with the official seal. An improperly validated birth certificate, or a copy of a valid birth certificate without an original seal, is not acceptable in most instances. Keep all birth certificates in your safe-deposit box, permanently.

Certificates of marriage and divorce.   These documents never seem important at the time, but when you change your name on a checking account, a Social Security card, or a driver's license, for instance, you may need to show one or both.

Request marriage and divorce certificates, stamped with the official seal, from the County Hall of Records where you were married or divorced. Get your marriage certificate from the Marriage Records division and your divorce certificate from the County Clerk where the divorce was filed. There is a small fee for each copy. Keep them in your safe-deposit box, permanently.

Social Security cards.   Social Security numbers were once used primarily to enter the work force, but today they are required identification for many reasons that have nothing to do with employment.

Get a Social Security card for every member of your family, even newborn children and grandchildren. When you apply for one at your local Social Security office, bring your birth certificate and, if you're married, your marriage certificate.

Children under five need an additional piece of identification. It can be a baptismal certificate, an immunization record, or other medical card that proves the child exists. Children over five can use a school ID card or report card as additional identification.

Keep your Social Security card in your wallet, and the stub in your home file or safe-deposit box, permanently.

To change your Social Security card from your previous married name to your maiden name, you need a certified copy of your divorce decree and one piece of identification. To change your Social Security card to your married name, you need a marriage certificate and identification in your maiden name. If you prefer, you can have two surnames on your card, such as Smith-Jones.

If you lose your Social Security card, you need your birth certificate plus two pieces of identification to get a replacement.

Military discharge papers. You may not ever need (or want) to look at these papers again, but, on the other hand, you may have to prove the length and status of your military service to claim government disability payments, qualify for a real estate tax exemption, get a particular loan, run for public office, or be buried in Arlington National Cemetery.

If you misplace your original papers, request duplicates by writing to the branch of the military from which you were discharged. Keep your discharge papers in a safe-deposit box, permanently.

Passports. If you like to be prepared for an overseas trip at a moment's notice, you'll want to have a valid passport at the ready. At peak travel times, it often takes two to three weeks to get one.

You can get a passport application at your local post office, and mail it to a nearby federal passport office. (First-time applicants need a birth certificate or U.S. naturalization papers and two passport photographs.) If you're pressed for time, you can apply in person. Passport offices are listed in the phone book under "Federal" or, sometimes, "County Offices." Passports are now good for ten years (five for minors) and are easily renewed with a currently valid passport. Keep valid passports in your safe-deposit box or home file.

Wills. If you haven't yet drawn a will, read Chapter 9, Distributing Your Assets. Promptly.

We suggest that you give your attorney the original copy of your will, retaining only a copy of it for yourself. Never place the original in your safe-deposit box. If you write a new will, you should destroy the old one; this erases any doubts that the new will wasn't intended to replace the old one. And if a different attorney draws the new will, ask the previous lawyer to destroy the old will and/or any copies he holds.

Death certificate. A certificate of death is issued by the county registrar and signed by a doctor. After someone dies, make a written request for at least twenty certified copies of the certificate of death from the county registrar; you'll have to produce them for a multitude of reasons, from changing charge accounts and collecting Social Security benefits to making life insurance claims and filing final state and federal income tax returns. Remember to keep one copy permanently in your safe-deposit box.

If death occurs in a foreign country, contact the American Embassy.

Financial Documents

Bank account information. Keep all bank statements, canceled checks, loan payments, and credit card statements that were used in filing income tax returns for seven years. You don't need to keep canceled checks, credit card statements, and other financial records that don't document income tax returns for more than one year. Record all bank account information on the *Banking Information* (#2) worksheet at the end of the book.

Copies of loan agreements. Always keep a copy of any loan agreement that is currently in force. For income tax purposes, keep copies of previous, paid-off loans for seven years.

Stocks, bonds, and government securities. When you want to sell stocks or bonds, place them as security for a loan, or settle an estate, you'll need the actual certificates. Because they are difficult and time-consuming to replace, keep them in a safe place, like your safe-deposit box. You can also leave them with your bank or stockbroker if they offer safekeeping services. Regardless of where you keep the actual certificates, list your holdings on the *List of Stock Securities* (#3) and *List of Bond Securities* (#4) worksheets found in the Workbook section of this book, and keep them up to date.

Passbooks. Keep information in your safe-deposit box as long as an account is open.

Pension and profit-sharing plans. Normally your employer will give you an annual record of your pension and profit-sharing plan. Keep this in a special file in your safe-deposit box as a permanent record of your account. If you have an Individual Retirement Account (IRA) and/or Keogh Plan, keep these in the same place.

Taxes

The Internal Revenue Service recommends that you keep copies of your income tax returns and the canceled checks that apply to those returns for at least seven years. The seven-year period is the statute of limitations for returns that understate income by more than the allowable limit.

Insurance Records

Keep all of your insurance policies in the same place—and contrary to popular belief, that doesn't have to be your safe-deposit box. In fact, you specifically wouldn't want your life insurance policies there in case the box is sealed in the event of a death. Both your insurance agent and the insurance company have copies of all your policies, so if you've misplaced yours, ask them for a certified copy.

Keep an up-to-date record of your insurance on the *Current Insurance Policies* (#5) worksheet.

Real Estate

With real estate, the best rule is to keep everything—certainly everything related to property you own. That would include trust deeds, real estate notes, title policy, and mortgage documents. You should also keep a file of receipts for capital improvements. When you sell the improved property, those receipted amounts may reduce your capital gain and provide a tax reduction.

Record all your holdings on the *Real Estate Properties* (#6) worksheet.

If you rent, you don't need to keep rental agreements and rent receipts for more than three years.

Medical Documents

Medical records. Keep records of immunizations, booster shots, and information on all major illnesses and surgery for every member of your family. As a precaution, also note everybody's blood type and any food or drug allergies.

Medical receipts. These include bills and canceled checks for doctors, dentists, nurses, physical therapists, hospitals, laboratories, pharmacies, nursing homes, eyeglasses, and medical insurance, as well as transportation costs for medical treatments. Since these document your medical deductions on your income tax report, keep them for seven years for possible tax audits. If any medical care is the result of an accident or negligence by others, keep all receipts in case of litigation, or until the case is settled.

Autos

The registration and certificate of title proving your ownership are extremely important. Without them you'll have difficulty selling or trading your car. Keep the original certificate of title in your safe-deposit box—*not* in your car.

Divide the registration into its two parts, and keep the renewal half at home and the other half in the car. In most states it is illegal to drive with a copy of the registration; you must have the original.

Keep the car loan agreement and records of the loan payments for three years. If you lease a car, keep the agreement for the length of the lease. Retain car repair receipts for three years; they would be invaluable if you wanted to sue because of an accident or needed to defend yourself if someone else is injured due to mechanical failure of your car.

Safe-Deposit Box

It's crucial that members of your family know in which bank you have a safe-deposit box and where you keep the keys to it. You'll probably receive two keys.

On the *Safe-Deposit Box Information and Contents* (#7) worksheet, be sure to list where you keep both keys. You might keep one at home and one in the office, but don't keep both of them in the same place.

Also, list the people who have access to the box. Be sure those names are filed with the bank on valid bank signature cards and also that those individuals know they are authorized to get into the box.

You might want to consider forming a family corporation and renting a safe-deposit box in your family name. That way your safe-deposit box can't be sealed on the death of one of the principals; members of the family will have continuing access to the box, and you can keep whatever you want in it.

Power of Attorney

A power of attorney is an agreement that gives one individual the right to act on behalf of another. You can name someone to act for you in all circumstances, or just in specific situations. When you describe the power of attorney on the *Location of Important Papers* (#1) worksheet, name the people who hold your power of attorney and describe the limits, if any.

Powers of attorney are usually revoked after the death of the individual.

FAMILY STATUS

The *Family Status Record* (#8) worksheet holds all your family's vital statistics. Remember to update the information at every birth, death, marriage, or divorce in your family so the record is always current.

BANKING INFORMATION

The *Banking Information* (#2) worksheet provides a complete list of your bank account information. Be sure to note whose name each account is in— joint, husband, or wife—and whether it's in trust for someone.

MARKETABLE SECURITIES

Here's where you record all pertinent data about your securities, either on the *List of Stock Securities* (#3) or *List of Bond Securities* (#4) worksheets. Include government securities with the bonds. Remember to keep these worksheets current, and record all buy-and-sell transactions.

NOTES

The *Notes Information* (#9) worksheet lists the pertinent data about all notes due you or due others.

CURRENT INSURANCE POLICIES

This is the master list of your family's insurance. Although details of each type of insurance are given in succeeding chapters, keep this overall record up to date on the *Current Insurance Policies* (#5) worksheet.

LIST OF CREDIT CARDS

Credit card fraud is increasing, and not only from lost or stolen cards. Counterfeiters are manufacturing phony cards that can utilize your valid credit card number while the actual card is still in your pocket. It's increasingly important to keep a list of all your credit cards so you can notify the various credit card companies as soon as you miss a card or are charged for purchases you didn't make.

Use the *List of Credit Cards* (#10) worksheet, updating it every time you get a new, or renewed, card. Also note who else is authorized to use each card.

IMPORTANT ADVISORS

Knowing who handles your personal and business affairs is obviously important to your family, so give each person who should have that information a copy of the *List of Important Advisors* (#11) worksheet. It's also helpful to send a copy to each of your advisors so they'll know who the others are and how to contact them.

SURVIVAL KIT SAVVY

When you've completed these worksheets, you've made a terrific start on organizing your family records. But if you and your husband are the only ones who know where everything is, it won't help your family in an emergency. It's essential to alert your family to the worksheets in this book, and particularly to the *Location of Important Papers* (#1) worksheet.

We believe every adult member of your family should know exactly where you keep your important documents, and that you've provided a complete inventory of them. The way to do this is to give each of them a copy of the *Location of Important Papers* (#1) worksheet. If you have young children and no other family nearby, alert a close friend to the existence of this worksheet and where you keep it. And, of course, give a copy to your lawyer.

Once you've completed the worksheets, you've done the hard work. Remember to update these forms at least once a year, and send the current copies to your attorney. The continuing value of this book is in your hands.

PICKING YOUR ADVISORY TEAM

2

"There's so much you take for granted when you're married," sighed Julie, a family counselor who was widowed seven years ago. "I'm talking about things like doing your income tax or deciding whether to sell a stock. All of a sudden there's no one around to help you."

Julie's story was so typical of the women with whom we talked it was almost a textbook case.

Like many women who are widowed or divorced, Julie was overwhelmed by all the financial and family details that her husband had handled. Now she had to take care of everything herself—including dealing with attorneys, accountants, and financial advisors—just at the time she was emotionally least able to cope.

Julie ran into problems at every turn. They started right after Rob died when she turned to their lawyer, who was also a family friend.

"Naturally I expected him to settle the estate," she said. "And he refused. He was very nice about it, but he said he was also the lawyer for Rob's business, and there would be a conflict of interest. His obligation was to represent the company and not me. He told me I'd have to find another lawyer." She shook her head as she talked about the tangled events that followed.

A friend recommended an attorney, but Julie felt he didn't pay enough attention to her problems. For him it was a small estate. For her it was everything. "The chemistry just wasn't good," she said.

Then there was an added complication because the partnership agreement hadn't been completed before Rob died. "No matter how close the business partner has been," said Julie, "when your husband is gone, he doesn't feel the same loyalty anymore." It was an observation many women echoed.

"But the worst part," Julie recalled, "was having to sit in an office with a male attorney, a male accountant, and a male business partner—and their attitude was I didn't know a damn thing, leave it to them."

The memory still infuriates Julie, and it made her almost evangelical about women understanding their business affairs. "If you have the information, and the professionals see you know what you're talking about, they're going to treat you with more respect," she said. It's advice she gives to every woman who comes to her for counseling.

As if settling an estate isn't traumatic enough, financial advisors suddenly popped up everywhere. "Everybody is after you, no matter what your income is," said Julie. "I got hit by every charlatan in town after Rob died. People wanted to sell me all kinds of things, and they sounded wonderful. They think you've got some money and you don't know much—and they're right. It's overwhelming if you've never had to manage money before."

Many newly single women have no idea what they can afford to do, and what they can't. Others turn their assets over to money managers without checking credentials. Some women are lucky, some aren't.

One of the unlucky ones told us, "You sort of fumble and bumble around, and how do you know whether the financial advice is good, bad, or indifferent? It makes a lot of difference, it makes a hell of a lot of difference."

When you're widowed or divorced, your need for advice is sudden and acute. "No matter how self-sufficient you think you are, when you lose your husband, you feel lost and vulnerable," said Julie. "More than anything you just want somebody you can rely on who's going to take care of everything for you."

There are many fine, well-qualified professionals who will take your best interests to heart, and there are those who won't. Sometimes it's hard to tell the difference. We'll tell you how to make that important distinction in this chapter.

What's important is to pick *your* team of professionals—*your* lawyer, accountant, insurance agent, stockbroker, or investment advisor. You may want to continue with all your husband's advisors, or you may want to change one or more of them.

You'll want to be sure those advisors will now handle your personal affairs as well as they handled your husband's business affairs. Get to know your husband's attorney and accountant better. Meet his financial advisors and see if you feel a rapport with them. Don't inherit any advisor you aren't comfortable with.

EVALUATING PROSPECTIVE ADVISORS

If you want to make changes in this advisory team, or select new advisors, keep the following guidelines in mind:

- Choose advisors who work full time in their professions.
- Favor people who have attained professional designations in their fields

by passing proficiency exams. A title doesn't guarantee superiority, but it does indicate effort and study in the field.

- Be wary of using friends and relatives. Will you replace them if they don't perform satisfactorily? Would you choose them if they didn't have a special relationship with you? Are they complacent about their responsibilities because of their relationship?
- Select your advisors based on the clients they represent, particularly if they are people whom you respect.

Don't be reluctant to question potential advisors. The best way to see if they are right for you is to interview each one. You'll want to know their professional credentials and experience, and how their office functions. To help your search, you'll find two worksheets—*Interview Questions for Prospective Advisors* (#12) and *Advisor Evaluation Guide* (#13)—in the Workbook section of this book. Take them with you when you interview advisors.

Rate potential advisors on your feelings about them after your initial visit. For example:

How quickly do they return your telephone calls?

Do they treat your professional needs with respect?

Do you think they'll give you adequate attention?

Are you more comfortable with a large or small firm?

What is your gut feeling about them?

Advisors and Their Fees

When picking advisors, don't base your choice on their fees. First select professionals who seem most competent and with whom you feel at ease. Consider their fees last. In some instances, fees may be negotiable. And if you think the fees are out of line, discuss that with them directly. Sometimes it's in your best interest to pay more for better advice and services.

If a potential advisor offers to counsel you gratis, out of friendship for your family or a special relationship, reject the offer graciously. The principal advantage of paying your advisors a fee for their efforts is that you can change advisors when you feel it's necessary. And don't hesitate to do that if you feel you've made the wrong choice.

Also, in time, your own needs may change, and the reasons why you selected the advisor may no longer apply. You'll be glad to be free to rethink your needs and pick new advisors who fit your current requirements.

In all major decisions—and picking your advisory team is surely one—get as much advice as possible. The person who becomes a financial wizard by making rapid decisions is a storybook stereotype, a fantasy; smart and prudent people seek advice widely before making important decisions.

When you've chosen your advisors, add them to the *List of Important Advisors* (#11) worksheet in the Workbook section.

SELECTING AN ATTORNEY

When a wife inherits her husband's attorney, she is likely to run into problems. As Julie discovered, conflict of interest is a common one. In fact, in new circumstances, widows and divorcées often need altogether different legal counsel than they had before.

Whether you need an estate lawyer, a bankruptcy lawyer, or another specialist, try to select an attorney or law firm that specializes in the field in which your problem exists. A good corporate attorney may not be a good tax or divorce lawyer.

Locating Lawyers

You can find the names of attorneys to interview from several sources:

- Referrals from friends who have had good experiences.
- Martindale-Hubbell publishes and regularly updates a book that describes all law firms and rates some. Consult it at your local library or in the office of a friendly attorney.
- The local bar association; area law schools, which normally have a referral service; and lawyer referral services, often listed in the classified pages of your telephone directory.
- The local office of the National Organization of Women (NOW), which normally refers women attorneys.
- Your accountant or banker.

If you decide not to use a private attorney, you can get legal help from special organizations. For example, Legal Action Workshop is a national organization of attorneys who can counsel you at their various offices. They specialize in relatively short interviews and immediate advice rather than long-term client relationships. They also offer prerecorded tapes about specific legal problems such as simple consumer suits or divorce.

SELECTING AN ACCOUNTANT

If you think of your accountant as someone who only prepares tax returns, either you aren't utilizing your accountant's full talents or you have the wrong consultant. Your accountant should be not only your financial caretaker, but also your financial advisor.

Sometimes the financial needs of husbands and wives are not the same, which is most often the case when settling an estate. For instance, after her husband died, Julie was caught in a complicated dispute with her husband's partner. "Rob's partner wanted us to use the firm accountant to go over the records of the business, and that just didn't sit right with me," she said.

Julie's instincts were right. Even if you and your husband's accountant have a good relationship, there are many situations, especially in settling estates, when you'll be better served by an accountant who has no prior association with your husband's business. Don't hesitate to call in an independent CPA and really challenge what is going on.

There are several types of accountants, and in selecting an advisor, it's helpful to understand the field. Like an attorney, an accountant can be a general practitioner or a specialist in business affairs, tax matters, or financial investments. The highest designation in the field is a Certified Public Accountant (CPA). To become a CPA, an accountant must pass a national examination given by the American Institute of Certified Public Accountants and work for a public accounting firm for at least two years.

Public accountants (they are not *certified* public accountants) are now licensed in many states. Their only limitation is that they can't represent you with tax audits or in tax courts.

In selecting an accountant, first consider a CPA. His designation doesn't guarantee performance, but it's an indication of his seriousness and commitment, and he'll be able to handle all your financial needs.

Locating Accountants

You can find the names of accountants to interview from several good sources:

- Your local banker or attorney.
- Your state licensing or control board, which can certify the good standing of prospective accountants.
- Local and state associations of accountants for their referral services.
- If you don't require extensive experience, you can probably keep your costs to a minimum by calling an area university for the names of recent graduates in accounting.

Taxes, Taxes

You can get tax help from three types of professionals, depending on your needs:

1. *Tax Attorneys* frequently provide year-round tax planning and can represent you before the Internal Revenue Service if you are audited, and in a court of law to resolve tax disputes. Normally, they don't prepare tax returns, and aren't experienced in their preparation.
2. *Tax Accountants* prepare tax returns, normally provide year-round tax planning, and can represent you before the I.R.S. if you are audited.
3. *Enrolled Agents* also prepare tax returns, provide year-round tax planning, and can represent you before the I.R.S. They are proficient in tax matters but they are not accountants. They normally charge less than a tax attorney or accountant, and often advertise heavily just prior to April 15.

If you have your tax returns prepared by someone who is not your regular accountant, be sure you get the following information:

- Does the tax preparer belong to a professional association?
- Will this individual be around after April 15, in case questions arise about your tax return or you are audited? (An audit can occur anytime up to three years after you filed a tax return.) If this person is at a temporary location, get a permanent telephone number for future contact.
- Before you start, get an estimate in writing of the cost of your tax return preparation. If you are refused, you may want to reconsider doing business with that individual.
- Will the tax preparer pay your fees if his error leads to an audit, and any penalties and/or interest resulting from that audit? You'd be wise to get that commitment in writing.

Regardless who prepares your tax returns, try to have some continuity in tax advisors. In case the Internal Revenue Service audits more than one year's return, you'll be better served if one person or firm has been handling you for each of those years.

The Internal Revenue Service gives advice—by phone or at their offices—on tax matters. It also offers a number of publications about taxes.

SELECTING AN INSURANCE AGENT OR INSURANCE BROKER

Some people make a distinction between an insurance agent and an insurance broker. An agent can represent one or more insurance companies and can bind insurance coverage on their behalf; a broker represents the client and normally can't bind coverage for a specific insurance company. Most agents and brokers hold both licenses, and the distinction is minimal.

For both agent and broker licenses, the highest designations are Certified Life Underwriter (CLU) for the life and health insurance agent, and Chartered Property and Casualty Underwriter (CPCU) for the automobile and homeowner's insurance agent.

We suggest that you select one person to handle your life and disability insurance, and another for your automobile and homeowner's insurance. It's difficult for one person to be knowledgeable in both areas.

Deal with a professional who has been in business for a reasonable period of time. The turnover in this field, particularly in life insurance, is extremely high, and you want an experienced agent or broker who intends to remain in the business.

Locating Insurance Agents and Brokers

Some sources for names of agents and brokers in your area include:

- National Association of Life Underwriters, 1922 F Street, N.W., Washington, D.C. 20006.
- One of the local life insurance agents' associations in your area.
- The Independent Insurance Agents Association of America, 100 Church Street, New York, NY 10008.

- The National Association of Casualty and Surety Agents, 5454 Wisconsin Avenue, Chevy Chase, MD 20815.
- The local independent agents' association for property and casualty insurance in your area.
- The offices of any major insurance company.

After you've narrowed your choice to one or more prospective agents or brokers, you can contact your state insurance department to find out if those individuals are in good standing.

SELECTING A STOCKBROKER

If you have money to invest, the choice of a stockbroker or investment advisor is everything. It's particularly confusing these days because both of them now do practically the same things. Stockbrokers buy and sell securities, and may also sell life insurance or real estate syndicated partnerships. So do investment advisors. Brokers are paid by commission on each sale; investment advisors usually charge an additional fee, often a percentage of the total value of your investment portfolio.

With the vast and rapid changes occurring in the financial advisor field, it's hard to predict precisely who will perform what function. What's most important is to choose an advisor who has not recently converted from another area to this field. Find out how long your prospective money handlers have actively practiced their specialties, then check with a few of their clients about their ability to handle your specific needs.

The Security and Exchange Commission (SEC) oversees all of a broker's actions except his competence. You have to judge that.

The best test of any advisor is his performance record. And the best way to measure that is to talk with long-standing customers. You can also query a prospective broker or investment advisor directly about his investment record. He may be able to document it with a fund his firm administers.

We recommend that you only consider brokers who have been with their firms for at least a year. There is high turnover in this field, and the longer a broker has been in business, the safer your investments will be.

If you have any questions about the standing of particular brokers, query the Security and Exchange Commission, 500 North Capital Street, N.W., Washington, D.C. 20549.

The best way to select a financial advisor is to arm yourself with as much information as possible. Take financial planning courses at local universities or adult education schools. Book an hour's consultation with an investment counselor (many offer a free consultation hour). Check with women's organizations like NOW for financial workshops in your area.

TAKING CHARGE OF YOUR FINANCIAL LIFE

FIGURING YOUR NET WORTH

3

Do you know how much you're worth?

You might think that's an idle question since you're probably not up for inclusion in the list of the "Ten Richest Women in the World." But you'd be surprised how often you need that information—and how few people have it at hand.

Nan is one of them. Like many women, she turned a homegrown talent into a thriving business. Egged on by everyone who tasted her incredible lemon cake and triple chocolate walnut torte, she launched Nan's Fancies with a cake and coffee buffet, and a toast to America's sweet tooth.

Now she turned away from the large ovens, wiped floury hands on her apron, and pointed to the commercial kitchen in the shopping center storefront. "Do you know how much this cost?" she asked. "I couldn't have swung it without a loan.

"I'd always left family finances to Bill," she said, "but this was my own business and I wanted to do it myself." After all her careful research into health codes, packaging, marketing, and profit margins, Nan hadn't expected to stumble at her first stop, the bank.

"When I went in for the loan, and the bank officer asked for my net worth," said Nan, "I didn't know what he meant."

Except for the details, our friend Bonnie told a similar tale. "My rental apartment was going co-op, and the insider's price was too good to pass up," she said. "The loan broker told me to bring in my financial statement." Financial statement? Bonnie is an editor; to her, financial statements mean how many books were sold, and at what price.

"It turned out they wanted to know everything I own, and everything I owe!" Bonnie's eyes roll as she remembers the scene. "It was some mess getting it together in a hurry."

Actually, we know just how Bonnie felt. We recently had to prepare the same kind of financial statement when we wanted to consult a particular financial advisor whose clients must have a minimum net worth.

Whether you're borrowing money to start a business, buying a house or apartment, or just want to find out how much you're worth, eventually you'll have to complete a financial statement. This simply states what you are worth. It's a fairly standard document, but it looks complicated and imposing, full of terms that you may not find familiar or even understandable. Just the sight of it makes most of us throw up our hands in despair.

To help you tackle the unfamiliar, we've defined all the items that make up net worth. We've also included two worksheets for you to fill in with your own information: *Record of Assets* (#14) and *Record of Liabilities* (#15). This is the same information financial institutions request, and in most cases, you can submit it on these worksheets. If you can't, you can easily adapt them to the institution's forms.

Think of your net worth statement as a snapshot giving you a picture of your financial position as of a certain date. You don't have to write down the information on the same day, but it should all refer to the same *specific date*. Recording information about earlier or later dates can blur your financial picture. Even if you complete these worksheets well after your chosen Net Worth Date, use information and bank statements that are closest to that date rather than current information. Pick a date to use for all your financial information. Most people choose the end of a month, say March 31, or the end of a fiscal reporting period, for example, December 31. Always designate your net worth with that date, and record it as "Net Worth, as of (date and year)."

Evaluate each item, based on your total liability, as of your Net Worth Date. On a loan, for instance, figure what you owe as of your Net Worth Date, not the original amount of the loan. On such long-term commitments as rent, calculate the remainder of your lease.

If you compute your assets and liabilities at your own pace, completing the two worksheets won't be as burdensome as it may now appear. Besides, you'll find the answer to that mystery at the bottom line: What am I worth?

YOUR ASSETS

In a financial statement, your assets are defined as everything you own that has a cash value.

Cash

Cash includes the money you currently have on hand, in currency and travelers checks, as of the Net Worth Date. It also reflects your bank balances as of that date. For example, if you pick December 31 as your Net Worth Date, record the balance in your checking, savings, and bank money market accounts as of December 31. You'll get those statements in January.

Securities

These include money market funds, stocks, bonds, and mutual funds.

Money market funds.   Record their value as of your selected date, using your money market statement.

Stocks.   To compute the value of your stocks as of the Net Worth Date, check their value in the financial pages of your local newspaper on the evening of that date or in the next morning's financial pages. You'll find them in the New York Stock Exchange, American Stock Exchange, or over-the-counter market listings. If necessary, your stockbroker can help you with this information.

Bonds.   To figure the value of municipal or U.S. Savings Bonds, list them at their current value—not their anticipated value at maturity. Any bank can compute the figure for your savings bonds.

Mutual funds.   Record the value of your mutual funds as shown on the mutual fund statement covering your Net Worth Date.

Other Investments

If you have invested in certificates of deposit (CDs), compute their worth on the initial investments as of the Net Worth Date. Don't record the total anticipated interest because you may cash in the certificate before it matures, thereby forfeiting some or all of the accrued interest. For bank repurchase agreements, list the face amount of the investment, and don't include the potential interest.

Life Insurance

All whole or straight life insurance policies have a cash surrender value. That's the amount you would receive if you were to cash in the insurance on a particular date. You can determine this amount by checking the cash surrender value chart on each policy and computing its value as of your Net Worth Date. Be sure to deduct any outstanding loan you have against the policy. If in doubt about the exact figure, ask your agent or the life insurance company.

Notes Receivable

This is bank talk for money you have loaned to others that you're fairly certain will be repaid. Don't count outright gifts or bad loans.

Real Estate

You can get an estimate of the value of your real estate holdings from a local real estate broker, or a formal property appraisal from a real estate appraiser. Most banks can provide you with the names of several real estate appraisers.

If your property is mortgaged, the mortgage holder may have a recent appraisal and can supply its current value.

Autos and Other Vehicles

The current value of your cars, trucks, campers, and other vehicles is listed in the *Kelly Blue Book*. You can find it at banks, automobile dealers, and auto clubs.

Pension and/or Profit-Sharing Plans

Your current employer will know the value and status of your participation in the pension and/or profit-sharing plans. Ask him to evaluate your share as of your Net Worth Date.

If you invested in a pension and/or profit-sharing plan with a previous employer, and if any of those funds were not paid out to you when you left that job, add them to your present pension plan.

Keogh and/or Individual Retirement Accounts (IRA)

Your latest statements on those accounts will give you their value. If your selected Net Worth Date is not within the current month, use a previous statement.

Other Assets

This is a catch-all for any property, other than real estate, that has cash value. It includes your home furnishings and household goods, jewelry, furs, antiques, art, collectibles, and anything else you think has value.

It's difficult to place dollar values on some of these assets, since we tend to focus on what we originally paid for an item rather than its current depreciated (or appreciated) worth. As a general rule of thumb, you can evaluate the total personal property in your home at 40 percent (or less) of the value of the home itself. This is the figure generally used by insurance companies for household goods insured under a homeowner's insurance policy.

You may want to determine the value of specific items. Jewelry, furs, antiques, art, silver, and collectibles can be appraised by competent appraisers who will visit your home, if requested. Appraisers charge varying fees, sometimes based on the value of the property, their time, or sometimes a flat fee, so get several estimates. Your household insurance agent can usually provide names of appraisers.

The information and worksheets in Chapter 14, Property Loss and Other Accidents, will be helpful.

YOUR LIABILITIES

In a financial statement, liabilities refer to your debts. They include everything you owe.

Accounts Payable

This is money you owe others, such as bills you haven't yet paid. These would be purchases made on charge cards, credit cards, and charge accounts. They also include medical bills, utility bills, lease payments, alimony, and child support payments. The most accurate way to tally these liabilities is to figure what you are legally obligated to pay over the next twelve months.

For charge cards, credit cards, and charge accounts, record the total amount you owe, even if you may not be planning to pay it all in your next payment.

Report all other accounts payable from the actual unpaid bills you have on hand as of your Net Worth Date. Also, record other bills you have recently incurred but have not yet received as of your Net Worth Date.

Loans Payable

Contracts payable. This is financial talk for loans secured by an item such as a car or furniture; it is money you owe others under a formal contract. It includes payments for automobiles, furniture, and other installment credit obligations. It does not include bank loans or real estate mortgages, which are reported in the following category of Notes Payable to Others.

If you aren't sure of the current balance of any contracts payable (loans), contact the lender for up-to-date information.

Notes payable to others. These are normally loans based on your good credit. They include bank loans, real estate mortgages, and other notes, such as loans from credit unions, profit-sharing plans, or emergency loans from your pension plan.

With both contracts and notes payable, report your entire debt, including principal and total interest, as well as the total remaining balance on the loan (not just the installment due on your current statement).

Taxes

The taxes you owe—property taxes, and federal and state income taxes—are also liabilities. To figure your true net worth, report all taxes that you owe but have not yet paid for the current year.

To figure all property taxes, call the tax assessor's office for your municipality. If you have already paid any portion of your property taxes for the year—either directly or to a monthly escrow account with your mortgage holder—deduct those payments from your total annual property tax bill.

To record your state and federal income taxes, consult your last year's income tax return or your estimated income tax return for the current year. Your accountant can give you those figures as well as his estimate of your current taxes. Again, deduct from the total any payments you have already made for the current year, including taxes withheld by your employer.

YOUR NET WORTH

You net worth is everything you own minus your debts. To determine it, just subtract your total liabilities from your total assets.

It's a good idea to compute your net worth annually. You'll find it useful in securing bank loans, in making up household budgets, and in evaluating your assets for a disability plan. You'll see how your assets and liabilities are distributed, and with annual evaluations, you can track the growth of your family's worth.

BANKING

4

"When I was young, I put my savings in a savings bank, and paid my bills from a checking account," said Janet, the office manager for a law firm in Houston. "After I started working, my husband, Al, suggested I open my own bank account. All I knew was I wanted a bank with an automated teller so I could get money anytime. Beyond that, there were so many possibilities and choices I didn't have the faintest idea where to go."

Most of us remember the simplicity of the good old days when you put your birthday check in a savings bank, got a mortgage from a savings and loan, a personal loan from the credit union, and bought securities from your broker. But managing money is a lot more complicated now.

"I didn't know if I should have a regular checking account or one of those special accounts," she said. "Or one of those money market funds that are at brokerage houses and now at banks. And I certainly didn't know the difference among them, anyway."

Vivian is a thirty-four-year-old schoolteacher we met in Chicago who had a different problem. She needed financial advice, and didn't realize that the good old-fashioned trust department of her bank could help. "I always thought trust departments were for widows or orphans," she said, "but nothing could be further from the truth. I discovered that by chance at the bank when I went in for some tax forms for my mother."

Vivian shook her head as she recounted her mother's predicament. "She doesn't have much financial expertise, and all of a sudden she had to make year-end financial decisions involving substantial funds. My father used to do all that, but his Parkinson's disease is getting worse, and now my grandmother is senile, so there's her estate, too."

At sixty-five, Vivian's mother is swamped by the emotional toll of a dying husband and a senile mother and these new financial burdens. She turned to Vivian, who didn't have the faintest idea what to do, until her chance conversation at the bank.

No wonder Janet and Vivian were confused. In the last few years, banks, savings and loans, and stockbrokers have been able to expand their services so widely that they often do virtually the same things. Today, you can buy securities at your commercial bank and write checks against your investment broker's money market fund. And all of that sometimes obscures the traditional services that banks still perform, sometimes differently than they used to. Add to that the changing nature of financial institutions, and even professionals are hard put to keep current.

In this chapter we've sorted out the main banking services, and give some guidelines on how to find what you need.

HOW TO CHOOSE AMONG THEM

There are four main factors to consider when making your choice: services, convenience, safety, and contacts.

Services. Although most financial institutions offer similar services, there are often important differences among them. For example, commercial banks, known as full-service banks, offer deposit, payment, and credit functions to their customers. Public brokerage houses ("non-bank" banks) offer a host of services but not loans. If you have children in high school, you might want a bank that gives college loans; if you're planning for retirement, you'll be interested in a bank's Keogh and IRA capabilities.

Detailed descriptions of basic financial services follow later in this chapter. The *Banking Services Checklist* (#16) in the Workbook section at the end of the book lists all the services you are likely to want. Use it to determine which institutions meet your needs.

Convenience. If you live and work in a small community where it's not inconvenient to have a checking account in one bank, a savings account across the street, and a market account at the local stock brokerage house, or if you don't mind banking by mail, you can utilize several different institutions. If it's more convenient to bank under one roof, use the *Banking Services Checklist* (#16) to compare the services offered by large financial institutions.

If you require a wide range of banking services but have few investment needs, consider a full-service commercial bank. For example, Al does all the family investing but Janet often needs money orders for her mother, and traveler's checks for trips.

One aspect of convenience is how quickly you have access to your funds. How long does it take local, in-state, and out-of-state checks to clear? How fast can you draw against your deposits?

Another aspect is ease of doing business. What are the banking hours? Do they meet your needs? Is there an automated teller system? Can you bank by mail? Are there Saturday or extended banking hours? The *Banking Services Checklist* (#16) will help you assess your needs.

Safety. Whichever financial institutions you choose, make sure they are insured. In the United States, most banks are insured by the Federal Deposit Insurance Corp. (FDIC), and most federal and state-chartered savings and loan associations by the Federal Savings and Loan Insurance Corp. (FSLIC). This means that deposits in each account in one name in one bank are insured up to $100,000. Note that a joint account does not increase the insured amount. If a bank fails, depositors usually have to wait some time before receiving their money, so having your deposit insured doesn't altogether eliminate potential problems.

Funds held by new financial entities—such as savings and loans, money market funds, and investment brokers—may or may not be insured by state-controlled insurance programs. Make sure the institution you are dealing with is insured.

In addition to insurance, check the soundness of prospective institutions. "In this era of serious questions about the stability of financial institutions, a look at your bank's 'statement of condition' or annual stockholder report is a good idea," advises financial expert Grace W. Weinstein, author of *The Lifetime Book of Money Management*. She believes a bank's accessible funds should be more than 50 percent of deposits and its net worth at least 5 percent of its assets.

Contacts. Any financial institution that has an established personal or corporate relationship with your husband will most likely be happy to help you with your financial needs. Ask your husband to set up a meeting with his banker. This should get you better attention and service. If the bank has a major business relationship with your husband, it may waive some or all of its service charges and fees.

Making Contact

Even if you have no special entrée to a bank, you'll get better service if you approach them in a businesslike way. Many women simply stop at the desk that has the sign "New Accounts." We think that's a mistake, though you could say to the person there: "I'd like to talk to someone who can discuss all the options your bank offers. Who could spend fifteen or twenty minutes with me to do that?"

Chances are you'll be directed to an officer of the bank or the branch manager. Officers and managers don't deal exclusively with corporations. They want to talk to people in the community. They'll steer you to the most knowledgeable people in the bank for your particular needs, whether it's opening an account, trust or loan information, or anything else.

The banking worksheets (#s 16–19) will help you evaluate competing institutions, their services, and their personnel. Clip them out of the Workbook section and take them with you as you interview various financial institutions.

BANK ACCOUNTS

Checking Accounts

Regular checking accounts.   These allow you to write an unlimited number of checks each month. If you maintain a minimum balance at all times, most banks provide free checking; otherwise, the service fee is minimal. Conventional accounts pay no or low interest on your balance.

Interest-bearing checking account.   Most banks provide free unlimited checking if you maintain a minimum balance (usually from $500 to $3,000) in this type of account. If your balance dips below the minimum, the bank levies a service fee that is usually minimal. An interest-bearing account pays low interest on the balance you maintain. Consider this if you write a large number of monthly checks and don't mind maintaining the required minimum balance.

Money market checking account (sometimes called a market rate account). If you want to have readily accessible cash that still earns high interest, consider a bank's money market checking account—it has a variety of names (Super Now is one of them). Its rates compete with the yield from money market mutual funds, but, unlike them, it is federally insured. The bank requires a minimum balance (usually $2,500), and if the balance falls below the minimum, it pays lower prevailing interest rates. You can only write three to five checks a month, although you can withdraw any amount of cash from the account at any time. If you write a lot of checks a month, open a regular or special checking account and replenish it from a money market checking account.

Money market mutual fund.   Technically, these funds are not bank accounts because they are managed by stock brokerage firms, not banks, but they offer many attractive features to compete with a bank's money market checking account. For the same liquidity, comparable or higher interest rates, you can write unlimited checks (some funds require a $250 or $500 minimum, others none at all). Initial deposits may range from no minimum to $250 to $2,500. The funds are not federally insured, although some are privately insured. Brokerage houses often offer several funds, with different features. For example, Merrill Lynch has six funds, including a Cash Management Account and Ready Assets. Most of these accounts are listed with their current rates in the *Wall Street Journal* and in the business section of most daily newspapers.

Savings Accounts

Passbook account.   All banks and savings and loans still offer the familiar passbook savings account. These return low interest, and don't offer any benefits. If you're loyal to a passbook account, at least be sure it compounds interest daily, from day of deposit to day of withdrawal.

Trust account. You can open this type of account "in trust for" someone else (usually a child), who receives the money at your death. Meanwhile, you pay taxes on the interest, and you can change the beneficiary and close the account at any time.

Custodial account. This is similar to a trust account except that the beneficiary pays taxes on the interest, presumably at a lower rate than you would pay, and is legally entitled to all the funds in the account; you can't change the beneficiary or close the account.

If you're putting money aside for a child, say for college, a custodial account is useful for transferring assets out of your higher-taxed estate. As the custodian, you can invest a custodial account in a certificate of deposit rather than a lower-interest passbook savings account. (For other ways to transfer assets to your children, see Chapter 8, Planning Your Estate, and Chapter 10, Childproof: Protecting Your Child.)

Certificates of Deposit (CDs). These are a type of savings account that pay a much higher rate than a passbook account if you agree to leave your funds in the bank for a specified length of time. The period may range from seven days to several years; the longer you commit the deposit, the higher your rate of interest. You can withdraw the earned interest, but you will be charged a penalty on early withdrawal of the principal. Rates vary from bank to bank, as do the methods of computing the rate.

THE TRUST DEPARTMENT

You're in good company if, like Vivian, you think the trust department of a bank functions primarily after a death by administering the estate. "The trust department doesn't do any good once somebody's dead," explains Teri Wilder, an officer of the Bank of America. "You need to preserve the assets in advance."

As Vivian found out, trust departments can simplify your financial situation at any time. In addition to acting as trustees and/or administrators of estates, they offer two other services: custodial and investment management accounts.

Custodial account. This type of account provides convenience, security, and freedom from the recordkeeping details of a financial portfolio. The trust department will collect dividends and interest, exercise options, and furnish a complete record of all transactions for your personal investment and tax information. It distributes income and principal, and makes investment changes, all as you direct. You retain title to the securities, and can amend or terminate the account at any time.

Investment management account. This offers all the convenience of a custodial account, but includes investment advice. Remember that banks are generally conservative; they look to both preserve and enhance the client's estate, so they will balance safety against return.

The fees for trust department services are set by each individual bank, but generally they are all competitive. The fees you pay the trust department for financial advice, like those you pay to any financial advisor, are tax deductible.

TRUST DEPARTMENT OR FINANCIAL ADVISOR?

Why use the trust department of a bank and not an investment advisor or broker?

Many of the financial services overlap as banks provide investment services and investment houses offer banking services, but the trust departments of banks offer a wider range of services under one roof to people who are too busy or not sufficiently knowledgeable to take care of their investments.

Trust departments administer living trusts (see Chapter 8, Planning Your Estate). They manage real and commercial property, pay real estate taxes, and file for delinquent rent. They also sell certificates of deposit and municipal bonds. They have investment counselors, trust officers, and attorneys available for consultation, and they work closely with a client's lawyer and accountant. "We put everything together," says Kathleen Ethridge, trust officer with Santa Monica Bank. "We manage the whole."

To manage your account, trust departments usually require a minimum estate, often around $100,000, which may or may not exclude real estate assets. Many investment advisors have a similar, or higher, required minimum, although brokerage houses do not.

As with the advice given to those with investment management accounts, trust departments tend to be conservative "unless the client directs us otherwise," says Ms. Ethridge.

AN ENVIRONMENT OF CHANGE

Financial institutions are constantly developing new services and concepts to win your business. Take advantage of this competitive environment by regularly re-evaluating your needs and determining which financial institutions can best meet them.

BORROWING

5

At some point in their lives, many women need—or want—to borrow money or raise cash quickly. And that's when most of them discover they don't know how to do it. Three of the women we interviewed had the same urgent need and no idea what to do.

Kathy is a young teacher from Kansas whose husband, Dan, always paid the bills. Playing tennis one morning, Dan collapsed with a serious heart attack. After four weeks in intensive care, and four more weeks in the hospital, he was sent home and ordered to rest there for two more months—no pressure, no stress.

Dan is in his late thirties with an excellent job as a pension actuary. Since his future looked so secure, he and Kathy had stretched their budget the previous year and put all their savings into a down payment on a new home. Now Dan was confined to it, prevented from going back to work.

"It was a stressful period because Dan was chafing at the bit," said Kathy. "One day I opened the mail and, to my dismay, saw that a huge tax bill was due. At the time, Dan was the last person I could bother about it, and I had no idea how to come up with the money." Fortunately, Kathy discovered she could borrow from the cash build-up in Dan's life insurance policy.

Nan is a talented cook whose cakes and cookies had a mouth-watering reputation in her community. Through word of mouth, she was besieged with orders from friends and strangers. Sensing a business opportunity, she decided to open a small specialized bakery in a neighborhood shopping center.

When she went to the bank for a loan to buy commercial cooking equipment, she was surprised to find that the past success of Nan's Fancies and the list of standing orders didn't satisfy the loan officer. "The officer asked me what I was going to put up as collateral, and everything I suggested turned out to be in my husband's name," she said. "Except my jewelry, and he wouldn't accept that." Nan didn't get the loan until her husband co-signed it.

Margaret was recently divorced. Her husband took the sports car and left her the station wagon, but she decided she preferred the ease and low-cost mileage of a sporty compact. "I wanted to finance the car instead of paying cash, so I'd have some funds available in case an investment opportunity came along," she said.

On her first visit to the bank Margaret discovered she didn't have a credit rating, and was therefore not considered a good credit risk. "I couldn't believe it!" she said, outraged. "I always paid my bills on time—and I've been known to run up some pretty big bills." Unfortunately, Margaret never realized that since all the charge and credit cards were in her husband's name, he was the one with the credit rating, not she. She had to pay cash for the car.

Few people are financially savvy about raising money, let alone quickly. For women, particularly, it's unfamiliar territory. But borrowing is a skill you can learn. Preparation is the key. You have to be ready on two fronts: first, you must know what resources you have, and second, you have to know how you can use them. This chapter is a road map through that unfamiliar terrain.

The first step is to review your total assets. If you've completed worksheets 14 and 15, you're halfway home and the accountant and loan officer will bless you. If you haven't, now is the time. You'll need this information whether you go to a bank for a loan or convert any of your assets into cash.

BORROWING FROM FINANCIAL INSTITUTIONS

Three rules will ease your passage in the world of lending: First, speak only to a loan officer who has the authority to make the loan. Second, establish credit for yourself *before* you need it. You can do this by borrowing money from a bank *now*. Present a valid reason for the loan—this may include taxes, a reasonable vacation, or furniture, but don't tell the lender you are borrowing simply to establish credit for yourself. They usually won't lend on that basis. Third, be prepared to show you are a good credit risk so that the officer can justify your loan.

Basically, there are two different types of loans: those that require collateral and those that don't. A collateralized loan is secured by some type of asset, like the cash in a savings account, savings certificates, certificates of deposit, or stock in a publicly held company. With banks you can sometimes use other fixed assets, like a car or real property, as security, but usually not jewelry, furs, art, or silverware.

Secured, or Collateralized, Loans

To determine how much money to lend you on a secured loan and how to structure your repayment, the lending institution will evaluate the assets you put up as collateral. Some assets make better collateral than others.

Stocks and bonds.   These are the easiest type of collateral because the bank knows it can convert them to cash if you default on your loan. Banks prefer securities listed on the American or New York Stock Exchange, but will consider over-the-counter stocks. They will normally loan between 60 percent and 70 percent of the current market price of a stock, and a higher amount on bonds (depending on the type of bond).

Cash.   Strangely enough, cash is also a form of collateral. You can borrow against your cash, and still leave it in a certificate of deposit or a savings account. This has the dual benefit of leaving your savings undisturbed and establishing credit for yourself.

Real estate.   Because the bank must determine a value and doesn't want to be in the real estate business of selling the property if you default, real estate is a complicated collateral. When you offer your home as security, the bank or savings and loan will appraise it to determine if your actual equity in the property covers the loan you are seeking. Moreover, bank appraisers normally assess your property conservatively.

Real estate loans can also be expensive. To get the loan you usually pay "points," which can vary from 1.5 percent to 4 percent or more of the amount of the loan, depending on the prevailing economic climate. You might also have to pay for the bank's title policy. Real estate loans are time-consuming and often take six weeks to process, so they are not a good source of emergency cash.

Automobiles.   These are accepted as security for some kinds of loans by some financial institutions. Normally, you can borrow up to 70 percent of the *Kelly Blue Book* value.

Jewelry, furs, art, and silver.   Although not acceptable security at most banks, these will be considered by finance companies.

Co-signing.   This is a form of collateral. The bank will recognize the value of a co-signer's assets in granting you a loan. Be sure the co-signer recognizes his obligation if you default on the loan. Even though Nan's husband, as co-signer, was prepared to repay her loan, she repaid it herself out of her business profits (which also helped her establish her credit with the bank).

Keep careful track of all guarantees in the *Collateral Guarantee or Co-Signature Record* (#20) worksheet at the end of the book. You never know when you'll need this information.

Unsecured, or Uncollateralized, Loans

Obviously, the stronger your credit position with a bank, the less likely you are to need collateral for a loan. (See Chapter 6, Establishing Credit, for how and why to establish a credit rating.)

If you're seeking an unsecured loan, you must justify your ability to repay it. Be prepared to reassure the lender with strong answers to these questions:

Do you have a steady income?

How long have you worked at that job?

Do you have a credit history?

Did you repay previous loans satisfactorily?

What is your repayment record with department stores and credit cards?

Note: A common misconception is that you must have a job to qualify for a loan. A woman can get a loan based on her husband's income, although he may have to co-sign the loan agreement. This loan can be either secured or unsecured, depending on his financial record.

Personal Guarantees

Anytime you or your husband apply for a business or a substantial personal loan, you will probably be asked to act as a guarantor on that loan. That means you'll be held personally responsible for any default on the loans if the original collateral is inadequate, and the lender can legally sue you for repayment. This differs from regular collateral because you are putting any and all of your assets at risk up to the amount of the loan, rather than pledging a specific item, like a stock or a bond.

This provision may seem harmless, but it could haunt you if you don't repay the loan because your personal assets—not just your business or corporate assets—are now vulnerable. Avoid signing a personal guarantee on loans if at all possible. Many times you have no choice; it may be the only way you can get a loan.

If you must sign a guarantee to obtain a loan, be sure to keep a record of exactly what you have guaranteed, and whether it is for your spouse or other family members. (This is important information for your heirs.) People often forget they have guaranteed a loan for someone else, only to end up making the payments themselves because the borrower failed to make them. Use the *Collateral Guarantee or Co-Signature Record* (#20) worksheet to keep track of these obligations.

Shopping for a Loan

Some interest rates for loans can be deceptive. Be sure to review the "Truth in Lending Statement" before you sign the loan agreement. This statement, which is federally required of the lender, clearly spells out the full details of the loan. When shopping for a loan, use the *Loan Interest Rate Comparison* (#21) worksheet to evaluate rates offered by competing lenders.

OTHER SOURCES FOR READY CASH

Bank loans are not the only way to raise cash. In fact, they sometimes take so long to process that you must turn to other sources if your needs are urgent.

The first step is to identify all your sources of ready cash. We describe the most common assets below, and divide them into immediate sources for cash and secondary sources where you can raise funds. Use the *Emergency Cash Plan* (#22) worksheet to lay out all your options.

Note: Get a power of attorney from your spouse (and anyone else who holds title to these assets) so you can convert them to cash in an emergency.

Immediate Sources for Cash

Checking account reserve. Decide on a minimum balance and keep that reserve constantly available in your account.

Overdraft account. If you don't already have an overdraft account with your bank, make arrangements for one. This account (it goes by different names in different banks, for example, "Redi Reserve," "Instant Cash," "Overdraft Protection," or "Automatic Loan Advance") gives you a prearranged line of credit on your checking account that allows you to write checks larger than your bank balance. You can get overdraft protection up to $5,000, depending on your financial strength and your relationship with the bank. You don't pay extra for this type of account if you don't use that feature.

Savings account. An obvious source of quick cash is whatever emergency reserve you decide to maintain in your savings account. Remember that certain financial institutions, particularly certain savings and loans, have time limitations on withdrawals. Be sure you understand those limitations so that these funds are truly available to you if needed.

Money market funds. A money market fund with a bank or a "non-bank" is an excellent source of liquid cash, and normally yields a higher rate of interest than a savings account.

Cashable securities. Stocks and bonds are another source for cash. If you don't want to sell your securities when you need cash, you can borrow 60 percent to 70 percent of their current value from a bank.

Credit card limits. Each of your credit cards has an approved credit limit available to you. It usually appears on your monthly statements. Ask each credit card company how to qualify for a higher limit, even though you have no immediate need for it. This is an additional source of quick funds, although the interest rates are high. (See Chapter 6, Establishing Credit, for ways to get individual credit cards.)

Undisbursed loan.   Some banks will grant you and your spouse a joint personal line of credit by establishing what is called an undisbursed loan; the bank agrees to the amount in advance, activates the loan immediately on request, and charges interest only when it disburses the funds. You'll probably pay the prevailing rate of interest at the time you need the money, but you have the security of knowing a sizable sum of cash is available in an emergency. You don't have to take the total loan at one time; you use whatever amounts you need incrementally.

Joint revolving line of credit.   If your bank won't give you an undisbursed loan, ask about a joint revolving line of credit. Like an undisbursed loan, you and the bank agree on the amount of future credit, but the bank reviews the arrangement periodically, usually every three to six months.

This type of credit has several desirable features:

● The interest can be based on a commercial rate, which is considerably lower than the rate for cash advanced in an overdraft account.
● You don't have to use the entire loan limit, but only the amount you need.

Secondary Sources for Cash

Secondary sources are not a lesser way of raising cash; they just usually take longer to get the funds.

Life insurance policies.   You can borrow on some life insurance policies, and the rate of interest is often attractively low. Ask your insurance agent for the cash value, if any, of your life insurance policies and those you have on your children. The type of life insurance you own determines whether or not this is a source of ready cash for you; if you have term life insurance, there probably isn't any cash value. (For a detailed explanation of life insurance and its cash value, see Chapter 11, The Role of Life Insurance.)

Ask your life insurance agent to send you the loan papers in advance so you can incorporate them in your emergency cash plan and, if needed, activate this source without delay.

Credit union.   Find out how you can borrow from your credit union. Complete all necessary forms in advance and put them in your file for the future.

Profit-sharing plan.   Check the terms for borrowing from your profit-sharing plan in an emergency. If certain forms are required, complete them in advance and file them for future use.

Personal loan companies. There are many reputable personal loan companies whose primary business is making short-term loans. Don't ignore them as a source of secondary cash, even if you already have a bank loan.

Car loan. If you have a car loan, ask the lender about refinancing your present loan. If he refuses, ask another lender to refinance the loan. You should be able to borrow 80 percent of the *Kelly Blue Book* value of the car. If you don't currently have a car loan, this is the time to get one.

Sell car. A car is an excellent source of immediate cash. Your bank or a neighborhood automobile dealer can determine its value in the *Kelly Blue Book*. Remember to deduct any loans you have against it.

Take a second or third mortgage on your home. If you already have a second mortgage, consider refinancing it with the present lender, or another lender, to get additional cash. Mortgage rates will vary with the current lending climate.

Change your state and federal income tax withholding amounts. You can reduce the amount of tax withheld from your paycheck and increase your net cash spendable income by changing your withholding amounts. If you're self-employed, work with your accountant in changing your tax estimates. Be certain you stay within I.R.S. rules to avoid any year-end tax penalties.

Pawn jewelry. This is a drastic step for a dire emergency. Before you take it, make sure you understand how to redeem the jewelry under your state's laws. With a pawn shop you can either borrow against the article you are pawning or actually sell the item to the shop. If you borrow, you have a designated time period to retrieve the item. During that period, you pay interest far in excess of bank rates but normally governed by the laws in that state.

Friends or relatives. If you're in a real bind, don't hesitate to approach friends or relatives for a temporary loan, but be businesslike. Formalize your arrangement with a promissory note that clearly states the terms of the loan, and how and when you will repay it. If you pay them a fair interest rate, you may feel less reluctant to seek their aid and they may accept interest-only payments for a specified period to help keep your initial obligation low.

Employer. If you or your husband have worked for the same employer for a long time and have a good relationship, consider asking him to act as a guarantor on a bank loan or to give you a personal loan through his business. Your selling points: the boss knows you can repay the loan through your employment (periodic loan deductions from your paycheck can be arranged), and relieving your mental stress will benefit your work.

Keogh or IRA accounts. Keogh funds have no loan provisions, but there are provisions for "hardship" withdrawals. You will pay a 10 percent penalty for premature withdrawal and you'll be taxed on the withdrawn amount.

You may borrow from your IRA account for up to sixty days without penalty, as long as you document both the withdrawal and deposit. If you borrow from your account beyond sixty days, you must pay a 10 percent penalty on the entire amount in the account.

As you can see, when you need to borrow money, the better prepared you are, the less you'll have to pay for it. Before you go for a loan, look over the worksheets for the chapters Figuring Your Net Worth, Banking, Establishing Credit, and Budgeting. You'll find them helpful.

ESTABLISHING CREDIT

6

Credit is like a passport. You never think of getting it until you need it—and then you're stuck until it comes through. Or, worse yet, you had it and you let it lapse.

That's what happened to Marlene, who in her single days had been an airline stewardess. "I had a good job, and it wasn't a problem to get credit cards and gas charge cards. But I made the mistake of letting them lapse after I got married."

Now, like a great many wives, Marlene doesn't have a credit rating. If you're in the same boat, it's probably for one of the following reasons:

- You didn't work before marrying, so you couldn't establish credit.
- You worked but you didn't bother to establish credit when you had the chance.
- You had credit but you lost it after you got married and failed to notify credit bureaus of your new name.
- You're a nonworking wife who doesn't have assets in your own name to support a credit rating.

It's not too late for you to rectify this situation. In fact, it's vitally important that you establish credit in your own name as soon as possible.

As our friend Margaret, eyeing a sporty compact, says (practically every day), "If I only had a credit rating, I'd have my new car and could unload this gas-guzzling monster!"

CREDIT AND WHERE TO GET IT

Credit is the ability to borrow money or to buy goods without cash. With credit, you can purchase goods and services from future income and you don't need to carry large amounts of cash.

In order to get credit, you need a good credit rating. You have to show that you're a good risk, that you—not your husband—can pay for the goods you've purchased and/or repay the funds you've borrowed, promptly and in full. It's harder to convince lenders that you're credit-worthy when you don't have an independent job or assets of your own, but it can be done.

The best time to secure credit is when you don't need it, because that's when it's easiest to get. It takes time and you should do it carefully. Here are the proper steps to take in order to establish your own credit rating.

Open Your Own Bank Account

Begin to establish your financial identity by opening checking and savings accounts in your name alone, not a joint account. And make sure it's your legal name—your legal name may be Mary Jones, Mary B. Jones, or Mrs. Mary Jones; it is not Mrs. John Jones. To get your own credit you need at least a checking account. Your bank accounts will not appear on your credit history, but they set the stage for future borrowing.

Pay the Household Bills

Put the utilities and telephone in your legal name, or at least in joint names with your husband, and pay those bills out of *your* checking account. This will help you establish credit, and it will avoid problems if your husband dies.

Take Out a Loan

If possible, take out a small loan with your local bank or credit union, even if you don't need the money. By repaying the loan promptly, you'll establish a good track record that will be invaluable for future credit references. Co-signing on your husband's loans won't help your credit rating. Make sure the loan is in force for one year so that it appears on your credit rating. Banks call this a "rated" loan. (Chapter 5 has more information on loans.)

Credit Cards and Charge Cards

Get credit cards and charge cards in your own name only, even if you and your husband already have joint cards. They are an inexpensive way of building your credit history because they carry no charges if you pay within a certain length of time. Moreover, cards held in joint names do not help you establish your own credit, and they may be canceled at your husband's death, at which time you might have difficulty securing new ones in your own name.

If you can't get a card in your own name, have your husband initially co-sign for you. This will still establish your credit. After one year, request that he no longer co-sign, since by then you will have established a credit-worthy payment record.

Pay all bills on all your cards promptly. The next year, request higher limits on your credit cards, even though you may not need it at the time.

Get both credit and charge cards. They are not the same, but both are excellent ways of establishing your credit rating.

Credit cards (MasterCard or Visa, for example).   These are primarily issued through a bank—unlike charge or convenience cards—and carry an annual fee and interest rates. Fees, interest rates, and finance charges vary from card to card and from bank to bank. Sometimes the same bank charges different fees and interest rates depending on the state in which you live.

All credit cards can charge varying interest rates, usually ranging between 12 percent and 24 percent per year, depending on the laws of the state in which they operate. With most credit cards, there is no interest charge if you pay within a specified time (about twenty-five days).

If the interest charges in your state are high, you can apply for a card from the same bank in another state. Write the American Financial Services Association, 1101 Fourteenth Street, N.W., Washington, D.C. 20005, for its Summary of Consumer Credit Laws and Rates.

Charge cards.   These are normally department store and gasoline cards. Unlike credit cards, with which you can secure cash, charge cards only entitle you to purchase goods and services from the company that issued the card.

Convenience or credit cards (American Express and Diner's Club, for example).   These cards charge fees that are higher than credit card fees, but bill interest or finance charges only if you pay late. Unlike charge cards, with these you are expected to pay the entire balance when it is due. Although these convenience cards allow you a few days grace, they will cancel your credit if you consistently pay late. A canceled card would be disastrous to your credit rating, so protect that rating by always paying on time.

Once you have received credit, request a review of your credit file annually from each credit source to make sure it's accurate.

YOUR CREDIT APPLICATION

An understanding of how credit is approved will help you improve your chances for a good rating. To see if you're a good credit risk, study the list of Credit Danger Signals on page 46. If your score is too high, change some of your spending habits before applying for credit.

Most credit decisions are made on the basis of the following questions:

Stability.   How long have you lived in the area? How long at your present address? Do you own or rent? Do you have a telephone, savings account, or investments?

Income. What is your occupation? Is it year-round or seasonal? How long have you worked for this employer, and are you paid by salary or commissions? (You must have either income or assets to qualify for credit.)

Debt record. How much money do you currently owe? How do you pay your bills? How often do you borrow, and for what reasons? (A declared bankruptcy or property repossession will be a major handicap.)

Expenses. How many dependents do you have? What is your life-style?

In considering these general questions, most credit or reporting agencies use their own system of scoring to evaluate your credit application.

If You Have Credit Problems

If you're notified you don't qualify for credit, or that credit is denied for any reason, take these steps:

First, call the person who signed the letter to make sure that no mistake was made.

Second, request in writing the reason for the denial. Look at the two sample letters, Request for Credit Information and Request for Credit Profile (pages 47 and 48), and use either to request the information.

Third, if you receive a poor credit listing, first find out the name of the reporting agency from the people from whom you are seeking credit—by law they must tell you. Then ask the reporting agency for a copy of your negative credit report—use the Request for Credit Profile sample letter. When you receive your credit file from the reporting agency, review it against the actions suggested in the Checklist for Your Credit File (page 49).

Finally, if you have already established good credit with a department store, bank, or elsewhere, ask them for the names of their credit agencies. Contact those agencies—most will be listed in the Yellow Pages under "Credit Reporting Agencies"—for their favorable credit report on you, and forward it to the company that has denied you credit.

Your Credit Rights

Under the Equal Credit Opportunity Act, no one can discriminate on the basis of race, color, religion, national origin, sex, marital status, or age. If you think this has occurred, you can make a formal complaint under the Act. If you need assistance, contact the Consumer Credit Counselor Organization in your area. This is a nonprofit organization supported by contributions from the business community, and it specializes in credit and debt counseling. You can also contact the National Foundation for Consumer Credit, Inc., 1819 H Street, Washington, D.C. 20006.

In addition, make use of the federal Fair Credit Reporting Act, which is helpful in keeping your credit records current and complete. Among the many rights you have under this Act, you can review your credit file at any organization at any time, know who received your credit report, correct information in your credit report, remove adverse information after seven years, and sue a reporting agency for damages.

As you can see, a number of government agencies will help you protect your rights. You don't have to face any of these problems alone, and in most cases, you don't have to hire legal counsel to do it for you.

CREDIT DANGER SIGNALS

		Yes	No
1.	Do you spend more than 40 percent of your monthly income on rent, condo, or mortgage payments?	[ ]	[ ]
2.	Do your credit payments exceed 25 percent of your take-home pay?	[ ]	[ ]
3.	Do you delay one bill so you can pay another?	[ ]	[ ]
4.	Are you receiving past due notices on any bills?	[ ]	[ ]
5.	Are you charging more each month than the payments you make on your credit accounts?	[ ]	[ ]
6.	Do you run out of money before pay day?	[ ]	[ ]
7.	Do you take increasingly more time to pay off balances on your accounts?	[ ]	[ ]
8.	Are you using credit card advances to cover everyday living expenses?	[ ]	[ ]
9.	Are you unable to save a little money each month?	[ ]	[ ]
10.	Do you use your charge accounts when you know you may not be able to meet the payments?	[ ]	[ ]
11.	Do you use credit cards to go on buying sprees?	[ ]	[ ]
12.	Do you depend on extra income such as overtime to get you through each month?	[ ]	[ ]
13.	Have you requested loan extensions from your creditors?	[ ]	[ ]
14.	Are you paying no more than the minimum on your charge cards or other bills?	[ ]	[ ]
15.	Have you ever made unrealistic promises to your creditors?	[ ]	[ ]
16.	Do you fear that your employer will learn the extent of your total debts?	[ ]	[ ]
17.	Does the size of your debts bother you?	[ ]	[ ]

If you have more than 5 yes answers, you have a major credit and spending problem.

FROM: _____ DATE: _____ 19____

_____

_____

Dear Credit Manager:

Please report all information concerning the account below in both of our names, as provided for by the Equal Credit Opportunity Act, Regulation B.

NAME: _____
　　　　　First　　　　*Middle*　　　*Last*

SPOUSE'S NAME: _____
　　　　　　　First　　　*Middle*　　*Last*

_____

NAME IN WHICH ACCOUNT IS LISTED (*name on the billing statement*)

_____

ACCOUNT NUMBER

　　　　　　　_____
　　　　　　　　　　　Signature

SAMPLE LETTER: REQUEST FOR CREDIT PROFILE

FROM: _____   DATE: _____ 19____

_____   FILE NO. _____

_____

Dear Sir or Madam:

Please send me a copy of my credit profile. The following is the pertinent information:

NAME: _____
            First   *Middle*   *Last*

SOC. SEC. #: _____

BIRTHDATE: _____
         Month   *Date*   *Year*

PRESENT RESIDENCE: _____

_____

_____

PAST RESIDENCES IN LAST FIVE YEARS:

1. _____

_____

_____

2. _____

_____

_____

_____
                        Signature

Check One:

[   ] Check enclosed.

[   ] I have been denied credit within the past thirty days as a result of information from your credit file.

[   ] There is an error in the information in my credit file.

1. Learn the nature and substance of all the information in your file.

2. Find out the name of each of the businesses (or other sources) that supplied information on you to the reporting agency.

3. Learn the names of everyone who received reports on you within the past six months (or the last two years if the reports were for employment purposes).

4. Request the reporting agency to reinvestigate and correct or delete information that was found to be inaccurate, incomplete, or obsolete.

5. Follow up to determine the results of the reinvestigation.

6. Ask the reporting agency, at no cost to you, to notify those you name who received reports within the past six months (two years if for employment purposes) that certain information was deleted.

7. Demand that your version of the facts be placed in your file if the reinvestigation did not settle the dispute.

8. If you are willing to pay a reasonable fee, request the reporting agency to send your statement of the dispute to those you name who received reports containing the disputed information within the past six months (two years if received for employment purposes).

BUDGETING

7

"There are women who have absolutely no idea how much money they are spending or what it costs them to live, and for a long time I was one of them," said Karen, a suburban Detroit housewife who works in a bookstore. For over a year, while her husband was sick, and then hospitalized, she struggled to manage the household accounts and write the monthly checks.

Karen's checkbook woes may sound depressingly familiar to you. "I didn't exactly manage the expenses," she explained. "It was more like muddling through. I'd get a big bill, like the semi-annual life insurance premium, and I'd put it aside, hoping to accumulate enough extra money from my salary and some dividends in time to cover it."

"Muddling through" money matters isn't acceptable to everyone, especially if you're trying to learn to handle your own affairs, as Patti was. Patti, the wife of a successful lawyer, realized about three years ago that she didn't know much about money management.

"All of a sudden I got nervous. I didn't know how to take care of myself or what it cost to run a house. When I told my husband my fears, he became very angry." Patti recalled his outburst. "He said, 'Don't expect me to teach you in a short time what it took me years to learn! Go and study yourself.' I guess I really touched a nerve by suggesting I wanted to be able to take care of myself," said Patti, shrugging her shoulders.

Eventually, Patti's husband agreed to set up a budget. Each was to keep track of and write checks for half the expenses. Patti recited the list of what she pays: the rent, the utilities, insurance, automobile repairs, her clothing, the kids' clothing, groceries, dry cleaning—all those kinds of expenses. "I write a hundred checks a month, and I balance the checkbook and keep track of how much is left in each category for the next month," she said. "And that's only half the checks!"

What bothers Patti is how little she still understands about budgeting, even though she puts in so much time at it. Paul pays for everything else, like travel. "A trip is a big lump sum of cash. How does he know there's enough money for that trip? I haven't learned to do that. I really still have no idea how much money we spend each month or what we can afford."

As most of us find out the hard way, one of the important steps in a financial education is gaining control of our own finances. We all have to learn how to manage those mandatory expenses we must pay for. A harder lesson is knowing what we can afford to do with our discretionary funds. In spite of Patti's bewilderment, budgeting is the best way you can learn. Budgeting helps you locate money you didn't know you had and direct it where you want it, as we show you in this chapter.

We know people despair at the thought of making—and sticking to— a budget, but you'll also discover there's an up side to what we agree is a tedious task. For one, a budget acts as a brake whenever you're tempted to overcharge on a credit card. For another, a budget will help you get a loan because it demonstrates to lending institutions that you have control of your finances. And best of all, for your diligence and discipline in budget-keeping, you may be rewarded by finding extra funds that you can spend any way you want—a budget bonus.

Budgeting Worksheets

The budgeting worksheets (#s 23–27) in the Workbook section will help you identify where you spend your money. As soon as you record your actual expenses, you'll see which ones are mandatory and which are discretionary. Then you'll be able to make thoughtful decisions about expenses you can eliminate and those you must pay.

The *Daily Cash Budgeting Worksheet* (#23) tracks your money on a day-to-day basis, so you can see where all your cash is going. List everything you spend each day; at the end of a week, evaluate your daily expenses and decide if you want to institute some controls over the cash. This will remind you to evaluate each such expenditure carefully in terms of your overall budget.

The *Monthly Expense Budgeting Worksheet* (#24) is for those of you who are really serious about budgeting and want to measure your expenses for one entire month before completing a working budget.

The *Annual Expense Budgeting Worksheet* (#25) tallies all your expenses for the year, and enables you to translate each item into an average monthly amount. Some of your expenses only occur once a year, some are seasonal, others are monthly. To estimate the monthly cost of items you pay annually, divide the total by twelve and enter that monthly average. If you have seasonal costs—such as swimming pool maintenance—or quarterly bills—such as tax returns for household employees—divide the annual totals by twelve to get monthly averages.

After you have completed the *Annual Expense Budgeting Worksheet* (#25) you'll have an average monthly amount for every item. Total those monthly amounts to see how your total monthly expenses compare with your total monthly income. If your income exceeds your expenses, consider where you want to commit more funds. If your expenses are larger than your income, review the worksheet to see where you can reduce or eliminate discretionary purchases.

The mathematics are simple: If you need, or want, more discretionary income, you must either increase your income or reduce your expenses. Cutting expenses is easier. By listing all your noncritical outlays on the *Discretionary Expense Worksheet* (#26) you'll be able to see how much you can pick up in each category and where you want to control your spending.

A *Monthly Budget Control Worksheet* (#27) will help you focus on your balance of payments. When you've decided how you want to balance your own budget, enter on the *Monthly Budget Control Worksheet* (#27) the monthly total of all discretionary purchases you plan to eliminate. By reconciling your intended monthly savings with your available monthly income, you'll get your monthly expense budget.

Once you've prepared a budget, start to pay the family bills yourself. Pay all of them, not just some of them. That's the only way you'll get a total picture of your family's expenses. To keep you on track, at least every three months measure your actual expenditures against your budget, and make budgetary corrections as needed.

III

PROTECTING YOUR ASSETS

PLANNING YOUR ESTATE

8

The car accident that killed our friend John and badly injured Betty taught us a good deal about getting our family affairs in order. As we tried to help Betty, it became evident that a lot of the financial problems she encountered could have been prevented by proper preplanning.

For instance, Betty badly needed some cash after several months in the hospital. "I tried to sell some blue chip stocks we were holding for an emergency," she said. "But my stockbroker told me that since they were registered in John's name, I couldn't sell them until they passed through probate. He said if we'd only owned the stocks as joint tenants, they would have come to me automatically."

Betty shook her head, finding it hard to believe that such a small change could make such a big difference. "When John bought the stock years ago, he never even thought about title of ownership."

How you and your husband own securities is just one item that can make a critical difference in a financial crunch. How do you own everything else? Who holds title to your home? Your car? In whose name are the bank accounts and money market funds listed? If your husband is part owner of a business, what happens if he wants to sell his share, or if he dies?

To our surprise, often the smartest businessmen are careless about the legal structures of their businesses, as we found out from all too many widows. Barbara was one of them.

Barbara was a young woman whose pleasant face always seemed clouded. And no wonder, when we heard her story.

Her husband, Jim, started a software consulting business. When it grew too big for him to manage alone, he took in a partner. They wrote a partnership agreement, but it didn't spell out what would happen if either of them died. They were both young, and the future seemed infinite.

Then Jim died suddenly of a heart attack. The loyalty Jim's partner had for him ended at Jim's death. Without a buy-and-sell agreement, Barbara found herself in an adversarial position with a once-friendly business partner who turned hostile and combative. The wrangle over the value of the company and Barbara's share was long and acrimonious, and it cost Barbara more than she could afford. After a year with no resolution, she lost her house and had to move to a small apartment with her two young children.

"If Jim had worked out a buy-and-sell agreement with his partner—in writing—my life would be drastically different from what it is right now," she said bitterly.

Sadly, what happened to Barbara and Betty is quite common. But it doesn't have to happen to you.

No matter how big or little it is, everyone has an estate. It consists of all your possessions—not just everything you own, but also everything you owe. You're selling your family short if you don't try to protect it.

In this chapter and the next, you'll get a brief overview of how to safeguard your estate, and how to plan for its distribution. We will deal with probate—a court procedure that changes the legal ownership of your property after you die and makes sure your will is valid and your assets are properly distributed. It's an expensive, inconvenient, and lengthy process you may want to avoid. You'll also find valuable suggestions for the financial security of your children. You may not be an estate planner after you read these two chapters, but the *List of Ownership of Assets* (#28) and the *Estate Planning Checklist* (#29) will provide you with sound questions and organized information that will enable your advisors to do their best for you.

THE MANY WAYS OF OWNERSHIP

As Betty discovered, how you own your property may determine how your assets will pass, and to whom, on the death of the owner.

You and your husband can own (hold title) to property in various ways, each of which has benefits and/or consequences for you.

Separate property. This is property owned solely by one person. You can sell it, give it away, or will it to anyone at any time without the consent or permission of anyone else.

Joint tenancy. This involves ownership by two or more individuals. If you're a joint tenant, you have an equal, undivided share with the other joint tenants during your lifetime. As a joint tenant, you may sell or give away your share, but you may not will it away. If a joint tenant dies, that share automatically passes to the other joint tenants without having to pass through probate.

Tenancy in common. This also involves two or more owners, but each owner doesn't necessarily have an equal share. As a tenant in common, you may sell, give, or will your share of the property without the consent of the other tenants in common.

Community property.   A form of ownership that exists in eight states, this is property acquired during marriage. During your lifetime, neither you nor your husband may sell or give away any of the community property without the other's consent. But on death, either of you can will away your half of the community property; the other half belongs to the survivor.

All gifts or inheritances you receive are separate from your community property, and if you want to keep them separate, be sure they don't get mixed up with community property, or they'll be presumed to be community.

There are tax advantages to community property ownership. When either you or your husband dies, the tax basis for both halves of the community property is raised to current market value, reducing the capital gains tax.

On the *List of Ownership of Assets* (#28) worksheet, located in the Workbook section, record the way in which all your family property is owned. It will help your lawyer and accountant coordinate your tax and estate planning needs.

BUY-AND-SELL AGREEMENTS

Even though participation in a business is often the biggest asset a husband has, inexplicably all too many businessmen don't have buy-and-sell agreements with their partners or their company. This agreement should spell out precisely what happens when a participant wants to sell his share, or if he dies or is disabled. The absence of such an agreement is a profound oversight that leaves you vulnerable to financial difficulties. Don't let that happen to you.

Even if you don't have a problem with your husband's partner, you will certainly have to confront a different adversary—the Internal Revenue Service. Without a valid buy-and-sell agreement, the I.R.S. will set a value on the business to determine the estate tax. Your husband, with his partners, should establish the value of the business, rather than leave you to negotiate with the I.R.S. after he's dead.

Encourage your husband to initiate or update a buy-and-sell agreement—and make sure it applies to disability as well as death. This agreement is just as important to your husband's partner, because any agreement that protects you will protect his heirs as well. It's the most professional and easiest way for each of you to receive an equitable share of the business.

Note: You can use life insurance to create a fund to cover a buy-and-sell agreement. The cash from the life insurance policy would immediately buy the other share of the business.

TRUSTS

"Thank God Bill set up that fund for the college tuition!" said Nan, the cook who started Nan's Fancies. "We never would have been able to pay for three kids at school—not at today's rates—if he hadn't planned for it when they were still in grade school."

What Nan was blessing was a Clifford trust, one of many different kinds of trusts that can solve a variety of your financial situations—if you know about them in time. For example, if you were as foresighted as Bill, a Clifford trust would take you over the unforeseen crest of rising college tuitions.

There are different kinds of trusts, each with advantages and disadvantages, and each meeting particular needs. You can set them up to take care of elderly parents, to control spendthrift children, or to subsidize your firstborn, who wants to write the Great American Novel. You decide how long they'll run, and who administers them. But for all their differences, trusts share certain characteristics.

Technically, a trust is a legal agreement between two parties—the grantor and the trustee—to hold, administer, and distribute your property for the benefit of your heirs. You, the grantor, name as trustee a family member, a financially astute friend, or a professional trustee, such as an attorney, an accountant, a bank, or a trust company. All trustees receive legal title to the property placed in the trust, and must follow the instructions you give in the trust agreement. Professional trustees charge an annual fee based on the size of the trust.

Trusts are complicated. You need an attorney who specializes in estate planning to advise you on the type that best fits your financial situation and objectives. But you'll help your advisors if you understand some common trusts and what they can do.

Testamentary trust.   These trusts are usually established to manage property for heirs who lack financial knowledge and experience. Suppose you want to name your sister as guardian for your children because she's the one who will take care of their day-to-day needs best, but she isn't capable of making investment decisions. For their financial care you establish a testamentary trust with an experienced money manager. You create this trust by designating it in your will, which means your estate must be probated before the assets can be placed into the trust by a court order.

Living trust.   The great merit of a living trust is that property placed in it doesn't pass through probate. It enables you to provide your family with funds for immediate expenses, plus an income upon your death. It protects the confidentiality of how you dispose of your property, and it minimizes court supervision over your property.

As the name implies, a living trust takes effect during your lifetime. Some you can end at any time, others you can limit to a certain number of years, or terminate at some event, for example when your children reach a certain age.

Generally, if you have a living trust, you also have a will that covers any assets not included in the trust. Your will and those remaining assets must go through probate.

A living trust must be either revocable or irrevocable. With a "revocable trust" you keep complete control of the property you put in the trust, and you can even act as your own trustee. You have the right to change the terms of the trust or end it anytime during your lifetime. Because you haven't relinquished control, the assets in the trust will be subject to estate and inheritance taxes.

In an "irrevocable trust," you give up control of the trust's assets and you can't alter its provisions for the life of the trust, which can run permanently or for a specific period of time. A major advantage of some irrevocable trusts is that assets are permanently removed from your estate, and, therefore, aren't subject to taxes on your death.

While recent federal tax law changes allow you to leave your estate, no matter how large, to your spouse tax-free, only a limited amount can pass to your other heirs without being taxed. An irrevocable trust allows you to shelter appreciating property that you want to distribute to your heirs and don't need during your lifetime.

Although the tax benefits of removing assets from your estate are appealing, the loss of control with an irrevocable trust makes most of us feel uneasy. You might consider one of several types of irrevocable trusts—sometimes called Clifford trusts—that remove assets from your estate for a period of time and then return them to you.

Clifford, or short-term, trust.   This type is commonly used for the college education of a child or to support an elderly parent. You transfer income-producing property to the trust for at least ten years plus one day. Your beneficiary receives the income from that property and pays the taxes on it, usually at a lower rate than you would have paid. After the trust ends or the beneficiary dies, the assets revert to you or your estate.

Q-TIP (Qualified Terminal Interest Property) trust.   This type of trust shelters its assets from estate taxes on a death, but is subject to estate taxes on the death of the surviving spouse. Its real benefit is that it allows you to provide for your spouse and still direct where your property goes after the death of the surviving spouse.

Charitable remainder trust.   If you own appreciated property that is producing little or no income, you might use it to create this type of trust. It allows you to give away an asset, receive an income tax deduction, yet continue to collect earnings from the asset until the trust ends—that would be anytime from twenty years to the death of your beneficiary or yourself. The I.R.S. will calculate your charitable tax deduction based on your age, the size of your gift, and your rate of return; higher rates of return receive lower deductions.

As you can see, establishing a sound estate plan calls for professional advice. Work with your accountant, an estate planning specialist, and your attorney—and to maximize their talents and minimize your costs, be properly prepared for your meetings with them. The *Estate Planning Checklist* (#29) is a handy review and a good way to get ready. You'll be glad to see that most of the information you need for it comes from other worksheets in *A Survival Kit for Wives.*

DISTRIBUTING YOUR ASSETS

9

If there's one act most of us postpone, it's making a will. Not only do we want to avoid an unpleasant subject, but we fear we're somehow tempting fate. As our neighbor Tom put it, "When I sign my will, I hear a loud thunderclap in my head and the gods say, 'Okay, now that everything's in order, let's zap him!' Let me tell you, when I leave my lawyer's office, I'm very careful as I cross the street!"

The only reason Tom finally updated his will is because he loves to travel. In an informal survey we once made among our friends, every one confessed they usually reviewed their wills just before taking off on vacation. As one of them said, "Listen, we worry enough about the children when we're away from home. At least this is one way we feel we're protecting them if the plane crashes."

In our heads, of course, we know that's nonsense. Not having a will can be dangerous to your wealth. The most disastrous consequences are excessive inheritance and estate taxes, and prolonged probate (we'll explain that later in this chapter)—not to mention the mental anguish that accompanies them. When you hear Julie's all too typical story, you may want to call your lawyer right away.

Julie is the widow of a successful Los Angeles accountant, and it was hard to believe she was the unintended victim of poor estate planning. As Rob's will dragged through probate court, Julie realized that, like the proverbial shoemaker whose children went barefoot, Rob was always too busy at the office to put his own financial house in order.

"For five years after Rob died I had no idea of my financial situation," said Julie. "I was living in limbo until the estate was settled."

Inadvertently, Rob bequeathed Julie two common and widespread problems: the agony of a long, drawn-out probate to settle the estate and excessive taxes that significantly eroded his assets. Careful planning could have reduced both the delays and the financial losses in distributing his assets.

How can you avoid Julie's painful predicament? A proper will, conscientious executors, astute trustees, and an understanding of the probate procedure will help you distribute your estate the way you want to, efficiently and prudently. It's worth your while—and your assets—to understand the process.

WILLS

Your will is a tool for distributing your estate the way you want it distributed. It is simply a written document that conforms to the laws of your state and explains exactly where you want your assets to go after your death.

Aside from this, a will can serve to reduce your estate and inheritance taxes and eliminate the extra fees and costs incurred when you die without one. The law gives you many choices if you make a will, but none if you don't. With a will there's a way—your way.

When you're considering how to distribute your assets, use the *Will Preparation Worksheet* (#30) at the end of the book. It will help you keep track of your beneficiaries and your bequests to each of them.

Types of Wills

Formal will. This type of will should be prepared by an attorney. He'll know what important provisions to incorporate and will discuss them with you. Your will must be properly witnessed by at least two disinterested people, who should sign it in your presence.

Statutory will. This is a preprinted form with standard wording approved by your state's legislative body. Normally, these provisions are rigid and any changes from the standard wording risk violating the state law on wills and invalidating the document. If you choose a statutory will, make certain that you use the most current form, and that you recognize its limitations. You'll also need two valid witnesses to sign the will in your presence.

Holographic will. This is a handwritten document prepared by an individual. If you make one, write it entirely in your own handwriting. You don't need to have it witnessed, but you must date and sign it. The margin for error and ambiguity is so great that we strongly recommend against this type of will. Moreover, not all states accept holographic wills.

Intestate is the term used when you die without a valid will. In that case, your assets are distributed according to the intestate laws of your state of residence, except for real property, which is distributed under the state laws where it is located.

A court-appointed administrator will manage and distribute your assets, and his decisions may be quite different from what you would prefer. Your estate pays the administrator a fee, normally 3 percent to 5 percent of the value of the estate, and the cost of the mandatory bond he must post.

Note: A *living will* is a document specifying under what conditions you wish life-support systems to be discontinued. It is not a legally binding will for estate purposes, and is not recognized in all states.

As your personal or financial status changes, you might want to modify your will to be sure it always reflects your estate planning goals. Review your will every year; whenever there is a birth, death, marriage, or divorce in your family; when you change jobs or retire; have significant financial gains or losses; move to another state; or the state of your health changes. You'll find a detailed listing in the *When to Review a Will* (#31) worksheet.

You can always revise your will, but never make changes on the face of the original. Any additions, deletions, or erasures on the document after it is signed and witnessed can invalidate the will and, at the least, may delay the settlement of your estate.

Your attorney can amend the will with codicils that explain, add, or delete provisions in your existing will. If you make numerous changes, he can draw a new will.

Give the original copy of your will to your attorney or the trust department of your financial institution, keeping only a copy in your home file. Do not store the original in your safe-deposit box; the box may be sealed at your death, causing difficulties in retrieving the will.

Mistakes to Avoid

Drawing wills is a technical skill you should leave to an attorney, but you can help him by being alert to some common pitfalls.

- Don't think you're covered by your spouse's will because you hold property jointly. If you both die together, say in an automobile accident, your jointly owned property might go to probate. If your spouse dies instantly, and you (the beneficiary) die a day later, you die intestate and your combined estates may fall under your state's intestate laws.
- Choose appropriate witnesses to your will. If your will is not executed by proper witnessing at the time you sign it, or it fails to adhere to the strict requirements of state law, your will may be declared invalid. If possible, don't choose witnesses significantly older than you who might die before you.
- Name alternate beneficiaries for specific gifts in case the primary beneficiary dies before you.
- Remember that your beneficiary—not your estate—pays taxes on your gift. You won't benefit the recipient of your Rolls-Royce if he has to sell it to pay the taxes on it. You can, however, shift the tax burden in several ways through proper planning.
- To avoid tax misunderstandings, ask the beneficiary of a gift to sign a dated receipt that describes it.
- If you want to exclude a spouse or child from your will, you must specifically state that. A spouse or child not mentioned in a will is called

a pretermitted heir. Because the law protects them from the oversight of the person writing the will, they have legal recourse unless they are specifically excluded in the will.

EXECUTORS AND TRUSTEES

Executors. You name an executor in your will to carry out its instructions. What your executor does is gather information about estate assets and liabilities, act as caretaker of those assets during probate, keep accurate records of transactions, and distribute the assets of your estate.

An executor also has investment responsibilities—for instance, preserving your property during probate and selecting the assets needed to pay taxes and other expenses of the estate. The job is time-consuming but temporary; it normally lasts from nine months to a year and a half.

For your executor, consider a close family member, an astute friend, a trusted professional, such as your attorney or accountant, or the trust department of your bank or other financial institution. Since the executor can be held personally responsible for errors, you may prefer to use a professional or a financial institution.

Naturally, make sure the person you choose understands the responsibilities and agrees to take them on. It's also a good idea to name a successor executor in case your first choice becomes unwilling or unable to serve.

Fees for executors are normally set by state, not federal, law, although it's sometimes possible to agree on a fee with your executor before your death.

Trustees. People often confuse trustees and executors. Your trustee administers whatever part of your estate you placed in a trust; your executor administers your assets that are subject to probate. The trustee's job lasts for the life of the trust, which can be many years; the executor is through once your estate is settled.

Your trustee's main job is to make prudent investments that protect your beneficiaries. Each state has laws that govern trustees and hold them accountable to the beneficiaries of the trust.

Whether you select a financial institution, a professional investment advisor, or an individual to be your one trustee, be certain they are skilled at managing money.

When you name your trustee, also name a successor trustee in case your initial choice for any reason cannot or will not serve.

Fees for trustees are not set by law. The trust department of a financial institution will normally charge a set annual fee or a percentage of the trust's assets. An individual trustee will charge whatever you agree on in advance, or, without a prior agreement, a reasonable amount set by the probate court.

When you interview prospective candidates, use the evaluation guides at the end of the book. *Evaluation Guide: Individual Executor or Trustee* (#32) lists the important qualities you should look for in an individual executor and trustee. *Evaluation Guide: Institutional Executor or Trustee* (#33) focuses on an institution's desirable strengths.

PROBATE

Probate is a legal term that can cause the calmest people to throw their hands up in despair. Technically, probate is a court procedure intended to change legal ownership of your property after your death, ensure that your will is valid and your assets are distributed to the people you name, and pay all debts against your estate. So why is probate so chilling?

- Probate can be tedious and frustrating, worse in some states than in others, and can drag on for months and even years.
- Probate is expensive. Your estate has to bear the cost of lawyers, accountants, appraisers, and the executor.
- Wills passed through probate become a matter of public record, available for anyone to read. Such public scrutiny may embarrass your heirs.

If you can plan your estate to avoid probate, your heirs will bless you.

How to Avoid Probate

Certain assets don't have to go through a will and, therefore, are not subject to probate administration:

- Assets held in joint tenancy and assets placed in a trust.
- The proceeds from your life insurance policy, which will go directly to the person or trust you name as your beneficiary.
- Most U.S. Savings Bonds, which go directly to the person listed on the face of the bond, if you haven't specified otherwise in your will.

There's also an alternative to the drawbacks of probate: Establish a revocable living trust, described in the preceding chapter.

CHILDPROOF: PROTECTING YOUR CHILD

10

"What would happen to your children if you were killed in an accident?" we abruptly asked a couple we were having dinner with. This is a topic that's been on our minds since our friends' car accident.

Elaine laughed. "'They'd probably watch MTV all day." But Len rolled his eyes—we had obviously hit a raw nerve.

"When we first made out our wills, my brother was married and starting a family right near us, so without even discussing it with him, we named him guardian," said Len. "We thought we were set, but he just got divorced, and he's living a bachelor's life—and loving it. We probably ought to find another guardian."

Elaine took up their story. "My sister, who's ten years younger than I am, certainly isn't capable of being a guardian to our children. And our parents are too old. We just don't know what to do," she said.

"Actually, we're thinking about our best friends—even though they live two thousand miles away—because they're just the best parents we know," she added. "It's awesome to assign this job to your friends, but we decided we'd rather have them than family. It wasn't an easy choice."

Elaine's right. It isn't an easy choice, but it's probably the most important one you'll ever make for your family. Curiously, most people make it haphazardly, and some people don't make it at all.

Even though parents spend a lot of time boasting about their children's exploits or moaning over their falls from favor or bicycles, most couples really don't spend enough time carefully planning for the fundamental well-being of their children. Very few think through that big question: What if a tragedy strikes and your children are orphaned?

There are a host of ramifications beyond the main choice of who will be in charge. How do your children feel about their new guardian? If the guardian lives elsewhere, as is likely, how will the kids feel about moving away? If you've chosen someone outside your family, how will your siblings and, more to the point, your parents, feel about it? In fact, how will your children feel about joining another family when they still have close relatives of their own? As Elaine said, it isn't easy.

Add to all this the increasingly common disruptions in family life: Grandparents move to the Sunbelt, far from children and grandchildren. Even if Grandma does live nearby, chances are she has a full life, perhaps even a full-time job of her own. In today's world, where divorce is frequent and cross-country job transfers almost as regular as commuter trains, very little stays the same. And the one thing we parents want for our children is stability and continuity.

Frankly, that's why we're dumbfounded when parents—and that includes many single parents—say, "The kids will be all right. After all, we have enough life insurance, cash in the bank, and a will."

What we've learned from many parents is that there's a lot more to protecting your offspring than money and a will. For example, even with the most trustworthy and thoughtfully chosen guardian, a host of problems can arise after one or both parents dies. Consider the following scenarios:

- The guardian you named dies and, because you failed to designate a successor guardian, the state appoints a new one.
- You place the bulk of your child's inheritance in an ironclad trust that can't be touched until he reaches a certain age; before that time his needs change dramatically, creating major financial problems for him.
- Your child receives the money you intended, but loses it through poor money management or divorce.

Naturally, you can't anticipate your child's future, but as caring parents you can try to guard against a variety of circumstances, foreseen and unforeseen, in your estate planning. Sadly, this is an area many parents overlook, perhaps because until now information has been sparse.

Good "childproofing" touches several issues: special provisions in your will and/or trusts, guardians, trustees, and—just as important for your child as for you—educating your child to financial matters.

WILLS AND TRUSTS

Since a will is the basis of sensible estate planning, we urge you to review yours at least once a year (see Chapter 8, Planning Your Estate). For the sake of your offspring, keep the following questions in mind during your review:

- Have any of your child's needs changed since the will or trust was drafted?
- Are the guardians, executors, and trustees still willing and able to serve,

or have any of them moved away, died, grown old, or in any other way become unsuitable?

- Have the tax laws relating to your children changed since the original will or trust was drafted?
- Are the provisions for distributing funds to your child still appropriate?

Handling Big Bucks

You know how well your children handle money, but if they are typical, they probably can't handle large sums responsibly until they are at least close to thirty. We've heard many a parent complain that funds distributed before then are often dissipated.

Moreover, with the high rate of divorce, you have to face the possibility that your child will be divorced. If your inheritance becomes part of the divorce settlement, it's lost forever, and your intent to provide for your child is lost with it.

For this reason, consider making partial distributions as your child reaches various ages: perhaps one-third at age thirty, one-third at age thirty-five, and the remainder at age forty. Or you could provide a certain level of income until your child reaches a certain age, when the remainder is distributed.

It's hard to foretell the future, but as you review your will and trusts, try to help your children weather potential emergencies. And if you've established a trust, give the trustee leeway to do the same.

GUARDIANS

A guardian is the person you select to raise your child if you die and if your spouse is unable, unqualified, or unwilling to raise your minor child. Normally, when one parent dies, the other parent becomes the guardian. You cannot, by will or otherwise, take this right away without good cause supported in a court of law.

If both parents die, someone must be designated as guardian. If you haven't made arrangements, the state will. As you can see, nominating a guardian is probably the most important provision in your will.

Types of Guardians

There are two kinds of guardians: guardians of the person, and guardians of the estate. And although most parents nominate the same person for both, the responsibilities are quite different.

The *guardian of the person* is responsible for the care, custody, and control of your child's daily life—and that includes food, clothing, and education. This person determines where the child will live and can authorize medical treatment. Naturally, you also want the guardian to provide the love and attention your child would otherwise receive from a parent. You may pay these guardians if you wish, but you should, if possible, provide funds for child care.

The *guardian of the estate* handles the business aspects of the relationship, including investing and managing the child's estate. When your child's assets involve complex financial decisions, you have good reason to choose a separate guardian of the estate. In many cases, the size of your estate will determine whether this special expertise is necessary. You customarily pay a fee for this service, either a flat fee or a percentage of the estate.

Selecting a Guardian

As you choose a stand-in for your most personal role—that of parent—you naturally seek a replacement who will be as caring, understanding, prudent, wise, and wonderful with your children as you are. To aid your search, two worksheets—*Evaluation Guide: Guardian of the Person* (#34) and *Evaluation Guide: Guardian of the Estate* (#35)—focus on the qualities you want for each job.

Also consider the following:

- Does the candidate have the necessary qualities—maturity, experience, temperament, integrity, stability—to be your child's guardian?
- Will a potential guardian understand the emotional needs and problems of your child?
- If you select one set of grandparents as guardians, will they have the stamina and patience for this role? How will the other set of grandparents feel if they're not chosen?
- Have you considered your candidate's age, marital status, other children, and, frankly, stability of the marriage?
- Will a prospective guardian have time for the task? Even if there are already other children? Even if both spouses work?
- Are you providing sufficient funds, or can the candidate take on this extra financial burden?
- Are your children old enough to participate in this decision? Knowing how they will be taken care of and by whom can allay the secret fears of many children.

When you settle on a candidate for guardian, understand that you only *nominate* that person; the court actually appoints the guardian. Nomination does not assure appointment, but it does carry great weight with the judge.

At the same time you choose your nominee, designate an alternate, or successor, guardian in your will in case the original guardian dies or is unwilling or unable to serve.

Professional Guardian of the Estate

If you feel uneasy turning over your child's estate to an individual, you can appoint a professional or corporate guardian of the estate, such as an accountant, lawyer, or the trust department of a bank. Normally, fees are based on a percentage of the market value of the estate or of the annual income.

Common Pitfalls in Choosing Guardians

- Parents don't consult with prospective guardians before naming them.
- Each parent nominates a different guardian (generally a member of that person's immediate family) in his or her will, which creates a tremendous problem for the court. Disputes burgeon if the parents are divorced.
- You choose co-guardians, commonly a husband and wife. This is appealing, but it raises problems if there is a subsequent divorce, separation, or death. In that case, the surviving guardian is responsible alone.
- You fail to provide for particular problems, such as medical or hospital care, that you know will occur.
- You aren't sensitive to whether the guardian can afford similar financial support for his children that you are providing him to spend on your children, and whether that difference in life-style will upset the guardian's household. You can remedy potential distress by offering to provide similar financial assistance to the guardian's own children.

Mandatory Guardians

If your children are old enough to take care of themselves but have not yet reached their legal majority, you may feel they don't need a legal guardian. However, there are circumstances where a guardian is mandatory. Here again, if you haven't selected one, the court will.

Some common situations that require a guardian are:

- When your child becomes a beneficiary under an insurance policy. (Most insurance companies won't pay benefits without a guardian of the estate.)
- If your child receives property under any kind of property settlement.
- If any liability claim is made against your child.

Guardianships of the Estate vs. Trusts

Before you settle on a guardian of the estate, consider the use of a trust instead. Ask an estate lawyer if a trust is a good idea for you. Meanwhile, here are some of the benefits.

- You can establish a single trust for all of your children; you need a separate guardianship for each minor child.
- With a trust you can set up a family "pot" to meet heavy expenses such as medical care for any child; with separate guardianships, you must divide your funds among them and hope that one child doesn't exhaust his or her fund.
- The guardianship of the estate of a minor child terminates by law when the child reaches majority. With a trust, you can postpone termination beyond legal majority, even until, if you choose, your child's death.
- If you are considering a trust, use the *Trustee Evaluation Guide* (#36) to assess potential trustees.

Once you've settled on your choice of guardians and trustees, list them on the *Childproof Protection Summary* (#37), together with the provisions you've made for each child in your will. As with all the worksheets, keep this summary up to date.

FINANCIAL GIFT-GIVING

One good way to begin to shift property from your estate to your children's is by giving them gifts. This removes those assets from your estate so they aren't taxed at your death and also lowers your own annual tax bill.

Each year, each parent can give each child a maximum sum without incurring any federal gift tax; in 1985, it was $10,000 a year, or $20,000 per couple. Moreover, you aren't limited to cash; you can also transfer securities. When these are sold, the profits will be taxed at capital gains rates and not as ordinary income.

If you want to encourage older children who work full-time to start IRAs, make your financial gift a full or partial contribution to it. Your children can take that IRA contribution as a tax deduction from their incomes—an immediate benefit to them.

HELP YOUR KIDS BE FINANCIALLY SAVVY

Handling money doesn't come naturally, and when children receive large sums through wills or trusts, most of them aren't prepared to manage their funds. It's your responsibility to give them a basic understanding of finances and of money as a tool. They'll appreciate soon enough the hard work it takes to make it. An excellent start is to include your children in the financial decisions that affect them.

Allowances

An allowance is a good step in your child's financial education. "Regular spending money is a preferable way to meet a child's needs, both his practical need for money and his emotional need for independence," says financial expert Grace W. Weinstein, author of *Children and Money*.

When you give your child a fixed amount—no strings attached—you give him the opportunity to make independent choices (both good and bad ones) and the chance to manage or mismanage his resources. An allowance teaches a basic financial lesson: If your child doesn't handle his money well, he'll run out. For your part, if your child exhausts funds before the next pay day, don't bail him out.

If your child regularly runs out of money, review the amount periodically, perhaps during a family budget session. Be sure it meets his needs, and agree on what it is to cover. And don't tie the allowance to your child's behavior.

Children and Work

In place of an allowance, or in addition to one, you may want to pay your child for performing specific household chores. Try to distinguish between daily tasks that you expect each family member to perform, such as picking up one's clothes, making one's bed, or putting out the garbage, and jobs for which you would otherwise hire outside help, such as cleaning the windows or washing the car. Our oldest daughter is glad for the clarification. She knows we expect her to wash the family dishes, but as soon as we have company, she's free to charge for her clean-up services—and she does.

By the time your children are in their teens we believe they should work part-time—and not at home. "The surest road to independence, to an understanding of real work and real earnings, is through work outside the home," says Weinstein. Whether it's baby-sitting, gardening for neighbors, working in a fast-food restaurant or retail store, or helping in the family business, children learn the meaning of work and money best at firsthand.

Bank Accounts

Start with at least a savings account, but, if possible, set up both savings and checking accounts for your children while they're in their teens. They'll learn to balance their own checkbooks early and may pick up a savings habit.

Credit Cards, Pro and Con

Credit cards are too hard for youngsters to handle, but some department stores are issuing charge (not credit) cards to teenagers. These have nominal credit limits and/or require a parent to co-sign; either way, parents are ultimately responsible for the purchases. A credit card of one's own—with built-in brakes—may teach one youngster good buying habits and responsibility for consumer behavior, but it can lure another into a buying spree. Know your child before you offer a credit card.

THE ROLE OF LIFE INSURANCE

11

For most people, buying life insurance ranks right up there with death and taxes: the insurance reminds them all too much of the former, and the premiums come with the regularity of the latter. They think—mistakenly—that life insurance is expensive and complicated to buy. And they can't figure out how much they need. That's why many couples, especially young ones, would rather operate on what we call the blue sky theory: Why carry life insurance? Nothing's going to rain on our parade.

That was how Carol, a young widow we met in Chicago, felt—until the sky fell in and she was drowning in the deluge. "When you're in your twenties and thirties, you don't think seriously of buying life insurance," she said. "You think, 'My God, we have all those years ahead.'" When her husband, Bud, died of a heart attack in his office, Carol had a twelve-year-old daughter, no job, and no life insurance benefits to cushion the blow. She had to sell their suburban house and move back with her parents until she found work and a small apartment. "It was tough that first year," she said softly.

Another couple in New York really validated our blue sky theory. Even though Peter had Hodgkin's disease virtually all through his ten-year marriage to Sally, they never considered life insurance.

"It was weird. It never entered my mind that anything would really happen," said Sally. "Even though we had children, life insurance was an expense we felt we just couldn't afford. When Peter's health began to fail seriously and he tried desperately to buy some, he couldn't get any," she added bitterly.

That's the way it is with life insurance (and most other kinds, too). Just when you need it the most, it's the hardest to get. If you have a policy and don't pay the premiums, the results are even harder to take, as one Los Angeles couple learned.

Vicki and Fred owned a real estate agency. Several years ago when they were short of funds, they let their one insurance policy lapse. Before they got around to buying another policy, Fred was diagnosed with terminal cancer. During the two years before Fred died, Vicki frantically tried to get insurance. She couldn't because Fred was "uninsurable." Then she heard about "open enrollment" policies, sometimes a way to buy life insurance without a medical examination, which we'll explain later.

"I picked up whatever open enrollments came my way, which is perfectly legal," she said. "That was the only kind of policy we could secure. It wasn't much coverage, but it took care of the bills those first few months."

Scrimping on life insurance is a common mistake of many young couples. It's too bad, because there isn't a less expensive way to safeguard your assets and prevent loss of income. Life insurance is actually among the best buys you can make. It creates cash, and it can generate an income for you for whatever length of time you choose. For example, a forty-two-year-old systems manager we know is buying $1 million worth of protection for his family for less than $1,500 a year.

After you read in this chapter about the different types of insurance, and how to figure how much you need, review your family's life insurance program to see if it will meet your needs. Too many women find out too late that life without adequate insurance is very hard indeed.

HOW MUCH INSURANCE DO YOU NEED?

That's always the big question. Most people feel they can't answer it without a crystal ball, but in fact you can make a sound educated estimate by using the *Life Insurance Worksheet* (#38) in the Workbook section of this book. This worksheet highlights your family's continuing financial requirements and suggests a formula to determine how much insurance you need.

First, estimate your immediate cash needs in the event of your husband's death. Would you have any debts to pay? Medical bills that wouldn't be covered by insurance or by your major medical deductible? Any other sizable amounts to disburse?

You'll want an emergency fund, and that amount is always difficult to project. The easiest way is simply to select a figure as a cushion, perhaps your living expenses for a year.

You also need to anticipate how much money, if any, you may need for federal or state inheritance taxes. Although the new federal laws will eliminate this for spouses, if you and your husband are in a fatal accident, your joint deaths may cause a tax problem for your dependents.

Second, figure your long-term cash needs. These will depend on the long-range financial plans you have already made, but don't forget that you still may want to create a retirement income, a savings income, and special funds for college or other family needs.

Third, calculate your monthly cash needs, using your budget worksheets

(#s 23–27). You know how much money you need today. How much monthly income do you want to provide for dependents? For any other household expenses? Use your best guess to determine those immediate future needs. Then multiply your estimated monthly budget by the length of time you want to cover.

Note: In estimating your loss of income, plan to replace at least 75 percent of it.

When you total your immediate cash requirements, your family's long-term needs, and the income for the monthly cash needs, you'll have a reliable idea of how much money you want to leave. You don't have to cover the entire amount with life insurance if you have other assets. To see how much your assets can reduce your life insurance needs, review Chapter 3, Figuring Your Net Worth, and worksheets #14 and #15.

In addition to providing for living expenses, you might also want to set up monthly allowances for your dependents, or give them each one lump sum. The place to list that is on the *Dependent Income Worksheet* (#39).

While you're reviewing your family's future cash needs, take the time to consider how much money and what specific assets you want to leave other people; note this on the *Beneficiary Worksheet* (#40). By correlating this information with your life insurance calculations, you can see if you're carrying sufficient insurance to do what you want to. This worksheet will also be helpful in preparing your will (see Chapter 9, Distributing Your Assets), and, needless to say, it should jibe with your *Will Preparation Worksheet* (#30).

WHAT KIND OF LIFE INSURANCE SHOULD YOU BUY?

There are several types of life insurance and various ways to buy them, so understanding your options will give you better coverage and probably at better prices. As you shop for insurance, keep the differences in mind.

Term Insurance

Term insurance lasts for a specified period of time, or "term"; it usually runs for one, five, ten years, or until a specified age, such as sixty-five. Its principal benefit is that it is the least expensive type of individual life insurance. Term insurance pays only on the death of the insured person and does not build up any cash value. Be wary of some term policies, known as decreasing term policies, that will reduce the amount of insurance annually; they cost less than level term policies.

A conversion clause in the policy is equally important. This lets you convert your term policy to a permanent (ordinary, straight, or whole) life policy without a physical exam, and is particularly attractive as you reach age sixty and term insurance becomes very expensive.

If possible, include a renewable clause that lets you extend your policy for additional term periods without a medical examination. Your premium will change (it's based on age), but at least you'll be able to maintain insurance even if your health fails.

Permanent Life Policies (Ordinary, Whole, or Straight)

This type of policy guarantees you coverage for as long as you live. The amount of insurance is normally at least the original face value, minus any loans against the policy. Unlike term insurance, permanent life insurance builds up a cash value over the years so that whenever you cancel your policy, you will receive the cash value that has accumulated. Moreover, you can use that cash value to pay your insurance premiums, borrow money from the insurance company at a guaranteed favorable interest rate, or as retirement income.

Because of the benefits of ordinary life insurance, its premiums are higher than those for term insurance. Its ultimate cost, however, may or may not be more, depending on how long you keep it and when you die. Some ordinary life policies also pay dividends that you can use to increase the amount of your insurance or reduce your next premium payment.

Universal Life Policies (Adjustable or Variable Premium)

Within broad limits, this type of insurance lets you determine the amount of your annual premiums. The portion of the premium above the cost of term insurance for each year is invested by the life insurance company and generates income, which stays in the policy and increases its cash value. You can withdraw these earnings and not pay taxes on them until the amount you withdraw exceeds the premiums you paid over the life of the insurance policy. You can raise or lower the face amount of the policy, which also changes the premiums.

Moreover, all along you receive interest on the cash value as it accrues in the policy, just as you would in a whole life policy; the rate varies with the insurance company. This "right" to redesign your policy each year lets you adapt your premiums and benefits to your ever-changing circumstances.

Group Life Insurance

Most employers now make group life insurance available for their employees, and pay part or all of the premium.

The first $50,000 of group life insurance is income tax free to you, but you pay a tax on higher levels of coverage. You may be better off buying individual life insurance if you want more coverage.

Group insurance is a nice supplement to your life insurance program, but it has its limitations: the coverage may be low, there is no cash value build-up, it stops when you change employers, and if it's not subsidized by your employer, it may cost more than individual coverage if you're younger than forty-five to fifty.

Open Enrollment

This is a form of group life insurance that some companies advertise in newspapers and trade magazines. You can purchase a few of these policies by mail without having a medical examination, although most programs require you to complete a brief medical questionnaire. The premiums vary with each plan, but are normally slightly higher than standard insurance programs.

Different groups, institutions, or associations offer open enrollment insurance policies to the public at certain "open" times. This is perfectly legal.

They can also be a life saver, as Vicki discovered. "When I was looking for open enrollments, I became an avid junk mail reader," she said. "I picked up one policy from a savings-and-loan association during a thirty-day open enrollment and another one that my stock brokerage house offered its clients with cash fund accounts."

The insurance companies expect people with urgent short-term needs to take advantage of the opportunity, so they often attach some strings. For example, a $100,000 policy might only pay $5,000 the first year, $15,000 the second year, $25,000 the third year, and not pay the full $100,000 until the fourth year. But as Vicki pointed out, "Even with the premiums, you'd probably come out ahead the first year. Five thousand dollars would pay some big bills."

SOME BUYING TIPS FOR LIFE INSURANCE

Changes in the insurance industry are rapid and sometimes dramatic these days. A good life insurance agent can give you current information. (See Chapter 2, Picking Your Advisory Team, for advice on choosing a good agent.)

- Select an insurance company whose policy meets your specific needs. However, if it's not a major, well-known company, check its standing with your State Department of Insurance or review its rating in *Best's Insurance Guide* (in your local library).
- Review all the life policies that you bought four or more years ago; the cost of life insurance has dropped dramatically and you may be able to find substantial savings.
- Also, review how you pay your premiums. Most insurance companies charge interest if you pay monthly or quarterly, rather than annually. Monthly "preauthorized check payments" (PAC) through your checking account can give you the ease of monthly payments without substantially increasing your costs. The charge for PAC varies with each company, but it's usually less than all payment methods, other than the single annual premium.
- Contrary to popular belief, almost everyone can get life insurance. Obviously, your premiums will reflect the state of your health, but you'll always find insurance companies that provide nonstandard life insurance coverage, even though it may be at higher rates for greater health

risks. These surcharged premiums will drop when your medical condition improves.

- *Never cancel an existing policy until you know you can obtain a new policy elsewhere.*

PLANNING AHEAD:
HOW TO HANDLE LIFE INSURANCE PAYOUTS

Normally, the proceeds of any life insurance policy are large sums. And they can present problems—and opportunities—in planning for their disbursement, particularly in how they are paid out, and in how they are taxed.

You can have life insurance beneficiary payments made in several ways:

- The insurance company can hold the proceeds and, for a specified period, only pay interest on it. This is called the *interest income* method.
- Payments can be made on a pre-determined schedule at a pre-determined rate. This is called *income for a specified period.*
- Payments can be made for the life of the beneficiary or beneficiaries jointly. This is called the *life income method.*

A word of caution when using any of these payment options: What seems like a good idea today may not be the best arrangement for your beneficiaries tomorrow. Consider the consequences carefully before designating any one plan.

ARE YOU MAKING THESE COMMON MISTAKES?

Putting your life insurance in your safe-deposit box?   In many states, that box is sealed at a death, and entry is time-consuming and tedious. Keep insurance policies in your home file so you can turn them in promptly for settlement. If you misplace them, get a copy from your insurance company.

Not naming specific beneficiaries?   A general statement, like "children of this marriage," won't do. If you don't clearly designate your beneficiaries, you may delay settlement of life insurance claims. A broad, but specific, description is best, such as: "All natural and adopted children, plus any daughter of my spouse." Whenever your family status changes—say you have additional children or a family member dies—update those changes on your insurance policy. Also, be sure your designation of life insurance beneficiaries agrees with the provisions in your will.

Naming your estate as beneficiary?   This raises the value of your estate because the proceeds become cash. They not only increase estate taxes, but also become subject to claims against the estate. You can avoid this by establishing a life insurance trust, which pays all life insurance benefits outside of your taxable estate. An insurance trust gives you all the normal benefits of your life insurance without any of the tax disadvantages.

Not insuring the wife? Husbands rarely consider the impact on family finances should their wives die. With working wives, it's the loss of a second income. If the wife doesn't earn money, there will be the cost of replacing her services to the family. Income taxes will increase because the family can no longer file a joint income tax return.

Designating the wrong owner? The owner of a life insurance policy is the person responsible for paying the premiums, and not necessarily the one who is insured. There are tax advantages to naming the beneficiary as the owner (the proceeds won't be part of your estate), but that can make it difficult for you to change provisions under the policy without the approval of the owner, and it gives the owner control over any policy loans or cancellation rights.

Relying too heavily on your employer's group insurance? When you leave that employer, you normally have thirty days to convert from the group to an individual policy, even though you may have become uninsurable. However, that conversion policy is expensive; the insurance company realizes that if you didn't have health problems, you would take a medical exam and get new insurance at a lower cost.

Buying additional insurance through your employer's group plan? Most employers furnish life insurance to their employees through a group insurance program. These group plans may also let you buy additional life insurance at your own expense. Normally, this is a poor purchase because the premium you will pay for the added insurance is higher than if you bought that extra insurance as an individual.

No "waiver of premium" clause? This clause forgives all future premium payments and keeps your life insurance policy in force if you become totally and permanently disabled. Adding this coverage to your policy isn't expensive.

Buying the accidental death benefit? This clause, sometimes called "double indemnity," pays double the life insurance benefit if your death is caused by accident. If you need greater amounts of coverage, you shouldn't depend on an accident to provide them. Moreover, the additional premium isn't cost effective.

Picking the wrong insurance company? The size and visibility of life insurance companies don't necessarily determine their financial stability or competitive policies. The cost of life insurance varies dramatically from company to company. Consult your life insurance agent, your State Department of Insurance, or *Best's Insurance Guide,* which rates companies on their financial stability and the quality of their management and is available at most local libraries.

Not reviewing your life insurance program regularly? Inflation and changes in health and family relationships all bear on your insurance needs. Make sure your policies keep pace with the rest of your life.

IV

HOW TO
SURVIVE
PRACTICALLY
ANYTHING

SERIOUS ILLNESS

12

Practically everybody has health insurance, but hardly anyone knows exactly what's in the policy. That can be perilous. Time and again we heard horror stories from women who assumed—mistakenly—that their families were covered under particular circumstances. Occasionally we spoke to someone who happened to be lucky.

Karen, a suburban Detroit grandmother, was one of the fortunate few. "We had taken out health insurance when we were first married, and never bothered to think about it again until Joe got sick," she said. "It had a $30,000 limit and a semi-private room rate of $20 a day. You can imagine how far that would go! At the time he got sick, the semi-private rate was $80 a day—and now it's in the hundreds."

Karen shook her head in disbelief. "It never occurred to us to ask the agent if our medical insurance needed updating," she said. "But by dumb luck, a month before Joe got sick he joined a group plan, which carried him through his illness. If we hadn't had that new coverage, I would have been in deep, deep trouble."

A family we met in Virginia wasn't as lucky. Tim is a salesman who changed jobs shortly before June's ulcer flared up. To their dismay, they discovered that Tim's new health insurance didn't cover a "pre-existing condition." They had to foot the bill for June's ulcer alone.

As if that wasn't bad enough, when Tim had a slight stroke several years later and was sent to a nursing home for physical therapy, the policy didn't cover that either. "It paid the doctors," June explained, "but because Tim hadn't been in a hospital for ten days before he was admitted to the nursing home, the insurance company wouldn't pick up the cost of the therapy."

Tim and June have since bought supplementary insurance, but it was expensive—and frightening—to find big gaps in their coverage. As June said, "You never know what surprises you'll find in your policy until you go to use it."

We sympathized with June, but we didn't tell her she was dead wrong. Insurance is one place you don't want to be surprised. As you can see, it's essential to know—and understand—your health insurance coverage *before* you use it.

Even if you know exactly what's in your policy, the cost of a long illness can be overwhelming. Vicki and Fred, the owners of a real estate agency, had a good family major medical policy that covered 80 percent of the costs. "When Fred was first diagnosed with terminal cancer, he spent a month in the hospital. The bill was something like $50,000," said Vicki. "Even though we only paid 20 percent up to a certain amount, it was very costly for us. I could see that if Fred had to go into the hospital again, I could run through my life savings in a hurry."

Vicki was savvy enough to learn about open enrollments—insurance you can get without a medical examination. When she bought some life insurance through a trade association, she discovered she could also get medical insurance the same way. Fred joined a fraternal organization for its open enrollment medical policy.

"We felt a little guilty about that," she said, "and we called the organization and told them what we were doing, but they said it was perfectly legal. Evidently, insurance companies figure on picking up people like us who need the coverage."

As you can see, there are usually ways to solve even the bleakest health insurance problems. But you'll avoid some agonizing moments and keep your costs in line if you have the right answers to these questions:

- Does your medical insurance keep pace with the rising cost of health care?
- Have you reviewed your coverage against prevailing doctors' fees and medical costs?
- Do you know how to cover yourself when you're between jobs? When you're self-employed?
- Should you and your husband each have a group policy?
- What happens to your medical insurance if you're covered under your husband's policy and he dies?
- In fact, do you even know how to analyze a health insurance policy?

We know this is a confusing field. Health insurance, with its wide range of coverages offering an array of choices, is far more complex than any other type of insurance you're likely to buy. It covers you in two major areas: medical expenses and disability income. In this chapter we'll review medical expense insurance; we'll talk about disability in the following one.

TYPES OF MEDICAL EXPENSE INSURANCE

You know that, in general, medical expense insurance potentially covers all your health needs, but when you review your specific insurance, it helps to understand that you can buy protection in eight major areas: basic medical care; basic surgical services; basic hospital expenses; hospital confinement coverage; major medical costs; Medicare supplement; accidents; and specific diseases. You may not want to buy coverage in every area, but you do want to know the impact of each kind.

Basic medical care. This covers your physician's costs for diagnosis and treatment of illness, including prescription drugs, X-rays, lab tests, and other services.

Basic surgical services. This pays a physician's fees whether he performs the surgery in or out of a hospital. Normally the policy includes a surgical schedule listing the maximum amount paid for each type of surgical procedure. In most cases, office visits directly related to the surgery will be covered on a limited basis.

Basic hospital expense. This covers your daily room and care, hospital supplies, and general services, such as X-rays, medications, and laboratory tests while you're an inpatient, with different limitations, depending on your policy. Some of the variables are length of a continuous hospital stay (usually from thirty days to one year), maximum benefit for each injury or illness, room allowance (semi-private or a maximum room rate), and miscellaneous expenses (normally limited to twenty times the daily room rate).

The basic medical, surgical, and hospital expense policies have a deductible amount that you must pay before your insurance coverage begins. The deductible, which may vary from $50 to $500, is applied each year against the expenses of each individual on the policy or, preferably, against the entire family's total expenses.

Hospital confinement coverage. This pays you a specified sum every day, week, or month you're in a hospital, with no limitations on how you use the money. These policies are normally sold by direct mail and supplement your primary health insurance policy.

Major medical. This is by far the most important insurance because it, more than any other kind, protects you against catastrophic loss from a major illness or serious accident. Its maximum coverage ranges from $50,000 to $1 million or more; at least $250,000 is advisable. If you buy less than $1 million, it's imperative that your coverage includes a clause for annual restoration of benefits so the amount of coverage isn't exhausted because of one claim.

Major medical always has a deductible; the higher it is, the lower the cost of the insurance. The deductible can be applied against each individual or, preferably, against the family's collective expenses.

Some policies specify a calendar-year benefit, in which you are reimbursed only for bills submitted during that year; if your illness carries into the next calendar year, a new deductible would apply. Other policies have a "per condition" clause in which benefits are not limited to a specific period of time.

Normally, major medical has a "co-insurance" feature that requires you to share the cost, usually 20 percent, with the insurance company. Some companies offer a "stop-loss" provision, which puts a ceiling, say $1,000 or $2,000, on your annual medical costs, after which the insurance company pays 100 percent of your bills (up to your maximum coverage).

Medicare supplement. This begins when Medicare payments stop. You are eligible for Medicare at any age if you have been entitled to Social Security disability benefits for two years.

Accident only coverage. As its name implies, this coverage protects you for an accident and not a sickness. Normally it covers all family members to the limit you select.

Specified disease coverage. This protects you against one or more named catastrophic diseases, such as cancer or heart problems, with a maximum amount for each disease.

It is possible—and quite common—to purchase these coverages in combination, such as basic coverage plus major medical, or basic coverage plus surgical services.

HOW DOES YOUR HEALTH INSURANCE RATE?

To see how adequate your existing medical coverage is, review it—and any policies you are considering—against the following questions. Record your findings on the *Medical Insurance Coverage Worksheet* (#41) at the end of the book. To see if you're getting the best buy for your insurance buck, complete the *Medical Insurance Cost/Coverage Comparison* (#42) worksheet.

Is there a "pre-existing condition" clause? This means that you would not be covered for any health problems you or your family had before the policy became effective. Sometimes you can have this clause waived by taking a physical exam that shows the condition hasn't existed for a period of time.

What is the maximum coverage your major medical policy provides? Is it for each illness, or is it cumulative for one year or over your lifetime. Is it for each family member, or for the family as a whole? If you can't get at least $250,000 in maximum coverage, consider an excess major medical policy with significantly higher limits. Since a serious illness can run daily hospital costs over $3,000, even that limit wouldn't cover you for three months.

What is the deductible amount you must pay before your coverage begins? Does it apply to each individual, or to the family as a whole? Does it apply to each new claim, or is it based on an annual calender year regardless how many claims you make in that year? You're better off if the deductible is applied once annually to the collective family's expenses and not against each person and each new claim because you would save money by paying fewer deductibles.

How does your policy define "dependent coverage"? Some policies insure all your children, including those away at school, or not living at home, while others restrict coverage to a certain age, usually eighteen or twenty-one. In most cases, your parents who reside with you are not eligible as dependents.

Is nursing care included? This would cover private duty nurses in a hospital when they are prescribed by a doctor. Sometimes that benefit carries over to post-hospital recovery at home.

Are nursing homes covered? Under what conditions? Can a patient go from home to a nursing home without a hospital stay?

Are you covered for maternity benefits? For any complications from a pregnancy?

Is there a "prevailing rate" clause for surgical fees? Are reimbursements geared to the customary doctor's fees in your area, or to a uniform rate? If you live in an expensive area, you want a surgical schedule that keeps pace with the higher fees you will probably be charged. If your policy is out of date, the insurance may not cover your doctors' bills.

Is there a rating formula that relates hospital costs to other expenses? The rating formula is normally one to three times the daily hospital rate; the higher the rate, the larger the allowance for other expenses.

Are you reimbursed for a second surgical opinion? Some policies, particularly group plans, now require you to get the advice of a second surgeon before undergoing a major operation. This doctor, approved by the insurance company, does not perform the surgery but warrants that it is necessary.

What does your policy specifically exclude from coverage? Many policies don't cover cosmetic surgery, dental work, or weight control specialists, or other procedures that may be important to you, except as required by a covered accident.

Can you convert your group plan to an individual policy if you leave your employment? Most group policies allow you to convert to an individual or another group plan if you act within thirty days.

What are the cancellation provisions? Some policies are noncancellable no matter what your health is; others are limited to a specific period, often one, two, or three years.

Is there a "guaranteed renewable" clause? This obligates the insurance company to renew the policy, but they can change the premium.

Do you have psychological coverage? This is not standard in a group policy, but can usually be added on an individual basis.

HOW TO BUY INSURANCE

Group Plans

If you're like most people in the United States, you're insured under a group program, either through an employer or as a member of an organization. Either way, you enjoy better insurance rates than you could get with an individual policy.

If you're an employee, your employer will pay anywhere from half to all the insurance premiums for you, but you're sometimes expected to pick up the cost for your dependents.

Since your employer or organization can change your group coverage at any time, review the policy whenever changes are made. Read the group insurance booklet your employer will give you, and contact the personnel department if you have any questions. Use the *Medical Insurance Coverage Worksheet* (#41) and the *Medical Insurance Cost/Coverage Comparison Worksheet* (#42) to monitor key provisions—for example, the exclusions.

If you're insured under an organization's group plan, you pay your share of the premiums, which are set by the insurance company.

If you or your husband aren't insurable and you belong to any organizations that have open enrollment periods in which you can buy medical insurance without a medical examination, take advantage of it.

Health Maintenance Organization (HMO)

HMOs are group plans, but they differ from regular group insurance in that they contract with specific doctors and hospitals to provide services to their clients. The doctors belong either to a group practice and offer care in a clinic setting, or to an individual practice association and see patients in their private offices.

Normally, an HMO offers the same coverage as any other group carrier, except for life insurance, which is sometimes part of a group insurance plan.

The advantage of an HMO is that it can usually provide comparable medical care at a lesser cost than you can get otherwise.

However, there are several features that may trouble you. You can't select your own doctor; you are normally assigned physicians by the HMO in your area, usually at one of their approved clinics, and, except in an emergency, you must use their services. This may be a disadvantage, if you travel frequently.

If there is an HMO in your area, your employer is legally obligated to offer you a choice between his group insurance plan and the HMO. Use the *Evaluating HMO and Group Insurance* (#43) worksheet to compare plans.

Individual Medical Insurance

You can buy any of the medical coverages we've described as an individual, either to supplement or replace any group or HMO format. In either case, carefully check what is and what is not covered; individual policies are often more restrictive than group plans. Look particularly at the pre-existing condition clause, cancellation and guaranteed renewable provisions, the surgery schedule, and the daily hospitalization coverage, including the maximum limit per day and the maximum amount for each hospitalization.

When you buy individual insurance, use an insurance agent who takes the time to explain all the details of the policy to you. (Chapter 2, Picking Your Advisory Team, will help you find a good agent.)

Large group insurers such as Blue Cross/Blue Shield also sell individual policies directly. They offer a variety of programs for individuals.

Direct Mail

Many hospital indemnity and accident coverage policies are solicited through direct mail and newspaper advertising. Although their coverage is too limited to use as primary insurance, they can nicely supplement your existing plans, and the premiums are attractively low.

℞ FOR SOME HEALTH INSURANCE PROBLEMS

You're caught between jobs, without any medical coverage at all.
Consider an interim short-term (usually six months) health insurance policy. It will cost more but it's better than nothing.

You're self-employed and not eligible for any group employment policy.
You need individual insurance, which provides essentially the same coverage as a group policy but costs more. Consider your local Blue Cross/Blue Shield, and commercial health insurance agents.

You and your husband are employed and are each covered by your employers' group plans.
If you are each paying insurance premiums, the one with the most restrictive policy should decline coverage. Two policies don't give you additional benefits other than covering your deductible, which will be less than the duplicate premium.

You're insured under your husband's group employment policy, and your husband dies.

Find out if his group policy covers you for a limited period of time after his death, during which you can get group coverage through an organization, or your own individual coverage. If not, get an interim insurance policy until you can arrange long-term health insurance.

A member of your family has a serious, "pre-existing" condition that requires expensive medical care and isn't covered by your regular health insurance.

Join one or more professional, university, or social organizations that offer group health insurance, or apply to Blue Cross/Blue Shield, during one of their "open enrollment" periods. During this time, usually a thirty-day period, you can obtain coverage without a medical examination. This is perfectly legal.

The benefits of your current policy don't begin to meet today's medical costs.

Ask the insurance company to increase the benefits, or buy supplementary coverage. But *never* cancel your present policy, even if it's inadequate, until your replacement coverage is not only in effect, but until the time limit for all "pre-existing conditions" has passed.

Purchase Hospital Confinement Coverage. It's helpful if you are hospitalized for a long time and invaluable if you are uninsurable for any reason.

As you can see, medical coverage is confusing and complicated. The options constantly change, benefits shift. Any misunderstanding about your coverage can have a devastating impact on your family finances. It's vital to your family's health, financial and otherwise, that you continually review your medical insurance.

DISABILITY

13

"When Tim had his stroke, we were so concerned about the medical insurance that we didn't even think about disability," said June, a pleasant woman we met in Virginia. "It was only a slight stroke, thank God, but even so, Tim was hospitalized for a month, and after resting at home, he was in a nursing home for a month for physical therapy. All in all, he didn't work for six months."

June's voice was tight as she recounted those months when she thought her world was collapsing. Her husband, Tim, is a salesman, and a large part of his salary depends on commissions, so there was a sharp loss of income. There was also the anxiety of not knowing if he could ever go back to work. As June reminded us, a salesman needs to be active and articulate, and Tim's stroke initially left him with a bad limp and slurred speech.

"All the regular monthly bills were coming in, and then, during Tim's lengthy recuperation, our new condo required a major plumbing repair and the property tax came due," she said. "The bad part was that I couldn't even go out to work. Tim needed so much help just doing simple things, like eating, that someone had to be with him all the time. It was either me, or hiring someone else—and I was cheaper."

June and Tim had to live on their savings, but eventually Tim recovered completely, and their ordeal was over in six months. A lawyer we know isn't as fortunate. He has Alzheimer's disease. He has limited disability insurance, and so far, his firm has been generous about carrying him. "That's going to stop soon," his wife told us. "I don't know what we're going to do then."

Most of us rarely consider the possibility that an illness or an accident will force us out of work for a significant period. If we're relatively young, we don't think of extended hospital stays, lengthy recuperations, or an inability to return to work for weeks or months, and certainly not forever. If we have good medical coverage, we feel well protected.

The cruel and frightening fact is that at some time many of us will be laid up and unable to go to work. It may be due to a multiple fracture on the ski slopes rather than a disabling illness, but whatever the cause, we may face a serious loss of income. With no paycheck coming in, we will watch our family's assets drain away.

There are two ways to avoid this financial nightmare: disability insurance, and an emergency disability plan. They go hand in hand.

DISABILITY INSURANCE

Disability insurance is protection against loss of income from injury or illness. There are three common ways to be protected: through Social Security, through your employer, and through an individual policy. Also, there are a few states that have disability protection.

Social Security.   No matter how young they are, Social Security provides disability benefits to anyone eligible for retirement benefits. Most people may not be aware they have this protection. Coverage for a permanent disability can begin with the sixth month, as long as you are expected to be disabled for over twelve months and you have certain Social Security work credits.

Although you may be eligible for benefits, there is a high denial rate and a substantial waiting period (often several months) for payments to start. Normally the benefits will not cover all your expenses, but they will supplement your other disability coverage.

State benefits.   Available in a few states, they vary by state and are limited; however, they do supplement other coverage.

Employment benefits.   These can range from a group disability policy to a specified number of sick days with pay. You may also be able to buy individual disability insurance through your employer's group health insurance policy; if so, seriously consider getting it.

Surprisingly, few companies have a formal policy on how many sick days they allow an employee annually. This is not a required benefit; in the absence of a clear policy, be sure to get individual coverage.

If you or your spouse are principals or partners in a business, disability raises another problem. What happens if either of you becomes totally and permanently disabled? How long would the business pay the salary? When would the other partners or owners want to buy you out? On what terms? A disability agreement is just as important as a buy-and-sell agreement is in case of death; work one out before the fact.

Individual disability insurance.   This is offered through a wide variety of plans whose benefits and limitations require study (see discussion below).

We strongly urge you to consider disability insurance if you have none, or review your existing coverage to be sure it's adequate. You should understand the important questions and definitions in this type of insurance, because it's all too common to have a disability policy that's inadequate when you need it.

How to Rate a Disability Policy

The major points in a disability policy are described below. Use them to analyze the policy you have or the one you're considering. Record your findings on the *Disability Insurance Checklist* (#44) worksheet at the end of the book.

How does the plan define disability? Is it the ability to perform your particular job or any job at all?

Payment of a disability benefit depends on your status as a disabled person. You can be totally disabled, residually disabled, or partially disabled because of an accident or sickness. Each category is covered differently, and it's critical that you understand the difference.

Total disability. In the newer policies, this means you are substantially unable to continue working at your job. Total disability benefits can cover you for your lifetime even though you are able to work in another field. However, some policies limit coverage to two to five years. For example, Henry is a surgeon; a spinal injury has made him a paraplegic. He receives payments for total disability even though he now teaches medicine.

Fortunately, Henry updated his disability policy before he had his accident. Under his previous policy he would have had to forfeit disability benefits if he worked in any occupation for which he was reasonably suited by education, training, or experience—in other words, as a teacher or consultant. Many policies don't pay total disability income if you work in *any* occupation. Moreover, some policies still require total in-hospital or in-house confinement to qualify for total disability. Make certain your policy is not that restricted.

Residual disability. This provides benefits for significant loss of earnings, usually after a period of continuous total disability. Normally you receive benefits as long as your earnings are at least 20 percent to 25 percent below your predisability income. For example, if Henry could teach or consult but no longer operate, or could only work part-time, his income would probably drop substantially more than 25 percent.

Partial disability. This provides benefits when you can't perform one or more of the important daily duties of your occupation but are capable of some type of work. If Henry can no longer operate but he can still assist as a consultant in the operating room, he would be eligible for partial disability benefits.

Does your disability insurance cover both illness and accidents?
Some policies cover accidents only, which is not enough. You must protect yourself against illness as well. Normally the length of coverage is lifetime for accidents, but a limited number of years (usually five) for illness.

Must you be totally hospitalized or house-bound to receive benefits?
Most policies let you leave the house or hospital for treatment without loss of benefits. You want the least restrictive definition.

How long must you wait before receiving payments?
A normal waiting period is thirty days, but some plans delay six months or a year before paying. Accident policies pay partial disability benefits immediately from the date of the accident.

How long do payments last?
This varies from a specified period of time to a total dollar figure.

What is the maximum monthly, annual, or total benefit?
Most plans range between 50 percent and 75 percent of your income. The payments are tax free, so the buying power is about the same as your previous taxable income.

Will another source of income (earned or unearned) affect your benefits, such as Social Security or Workers Compensation?
A majority of plans allow other sources of income.

If your employer carries this insurance, are the benefits based on your length of service or salary level?
Some plans require a minimum length of service (usually one or two years) or a certain salary level.

Can you convert your coverage to an individual policy if you leave that employment?
Most plans offer this option.

Is the policy guaranteed renewable?
This is an important safeguard if you carry individual disability insurance; if you're part of your employer's plan, you have no control over this feature.

Can you stop paying the insurance premiums while receiving benefit payments?
This normally doesn't cost more, but it's a feature offered by some insurance companies.

Can the rates be raised?
This is important because the cost of your disability insurance could go beyond your range.

Does a disability from a pre-existing condition prevent coverage?

If this limitation exists in your employer's plan, try to have the plan changed, make certain you get your own coverage without this limitation, or try to have the restriction removed by submitting a medical report or taking a new physical exam stating the condition no longer exists.

Is mental illness excluded?

Normally it is. Check the policy for its definition of mental illness.

How long will the survivor—normally the wife and dependent children— have continued coverage?

Usually, they have ninety days.

If there are any limitations in your employer's disability plan that make you uncomfortable, buy your own policy to either supplement or replace that plan.

TWO DISABILITY PLANS

Even if you have disability insurance, it may not start for several months after the paychecks stop, or it may cover only a portion of your expenses. To help you identify where you can get needed cash during that time, we've provided two worksheets: an *Emergency Disability Plan* (#45) to tide you over the first ninety days, and a *Long-Term Disability Plan* (#46) for your long-range financial needs. After studying the two plans (below), complete these two worksheets with your husband, and you'll have a sound emergency financial strategy you can activate if necessary. You may never need to use it, but you'll be comforted to know you're prepared.

An Emergency Disability Plan

This plan identifies three important areas: sources of ready cash, expenses, and emergency plans of action.

Ready cash.   This comes from primary sources, which is money already available, and secondary sources, which are funds you need to apply for. (You may find the information in Chapter 5, Borrowing, helpful.)

If you don't have disability insurance, or if you have any problem with your disability coverage, look over the many sources of possible funds listed on the worksheet to see what you may have available. Discuss each source with your husband.

For example, you and your husband may have a valuable collection you can convert to ready cash. A friend of ours, for instance, has race horses and guns. Because his wife, Priscilla, doesn't understand much about either, Jock prepared an emergency liquidation plan. "Jock wrote a list of which horses to sell first and where to sell them," Priscilla said. "Then he labeled his guns, and told me which to keep for their antique value and where to take the rest for consignment."

Expenses. These can only be estimated, but your budgeting worksheets (#s 23–27) will be helpful. Review them with a disabled family member in mind. Some expenses, like medical costs, will increase; others will decrease. If your husband is not at a local hospital, you'll have the additional costs of transportation, extra child care, or food for friends or relatives. Even if your husband is home, you may have to pay for chores that he did, like mowing the lawn or putting up storm windows. Try to project what new costs you'll incur and add them to your regular expenses to get a realistic picture of your cash needs.

We realize there's no way to estimate accurately what your expenses might total. Just being aware they may occur is one reason for keeping close tabs on possible sources of cash.

Emergency plans of action. Start with a review of your budget to see what expenses you can reduce or eliminate during this period. Knowing where you can cut costs is one key to managing during a disability; the other is the creation of immediate cash to cover necessary expenses.

Then list all your creditors whom you think might defer payment, or accept an extended payment period. Many creditors will be willing to accommodate you in special circumstances. No creditor wants to see you trapped financially and unable to pay at all. A sound creditor plan will stretch your dollars.

Notify the insurance company that issued the disability policy and recheck your medical insurance for exact coverage and deductibles. Then mobilize your support networks. We've listed some of these in the worksheet to give you an idea of the kind of action plan you can create, and to trigger your own thoughts. Assess your individual situation to see where you can turn for help and support.

Review your emergency plans periodically, and when your sources of ready cash or your expenses change dramatically, update the plan.

A Long-Term Disability Plan

This plan focuses on long-range solutions. It formalizes the temporary budget cuts of the three-month emergency period so you can put together a workable financial guide for the long haul.

On the *Long-Term Disability Plan* (#46) worksheet list your monthly disability insurance income. Then list any funds still remaining from your ninety-day emergency plan and any other continuing source of funds. Compare this total with your estimated expenses to determine how much, if any, you must reduce your expenses.

Now tackle a prearranged expense reduction plan. Using your regular budget worksheets (#s 23–27), decide with your husband what expenses you can reduce permanently, and by how much.

If you or your husband are disabled, after the first three months you may have an idea of how long the disability will last, and how you'll need to budget your funds. With your austerity income and expenses clearly documented, you'll be able to determine if your income covers your expenses and, if not, what the deficit will be.

At the time, you'll want to develop alternative sources of income to meet any shortfall. You'll want to consider full-time and part-time work, and, if you have young children, establishing a business at home. (Chapter 18, The Job Market, has helpful ideas and know-how.)

You may also have other income-producing resources: an extra bedroom to rent out, or a teenage child who can contribute to the family kitty by shoveling snow, baby-sitting, washing cars, or mowing lawns. Grace W. Weinstein, author of *The Lifetime Book of Money Management*, says, "Look to the earnings of other family members. Now, if ever, is the time for you all to pull together."

As always with managing your money, if your expenses and sources of income change significantly, draw up a revised version of this long-term plan.

PROPERTY LOSS AND OTHER ACCIDENTS

14

When you have something of particular value, like a piece of jewelry or a fur coat or a painting, most of us think immediately of insuring it. What rarely occurs to us is losing our everyday possessions—and that can be more devastating than the loss of a single valuable item.

At a business convention we met a woman from Chicago who told us the ultimate horror story. "We were moving to Connecticut, and when the movers looked at the contents of our three-bedroom apartment, they said, 'The standard insurance on this would be about $10,000. Is that what you'd like?' It sounded like more than enough, so I said sure."

Maureen figured that if the movers dropped a couch or damaged a cabinet, the insurance would certainly cover the repairs. What she never envisioned was a total loss. But an accidental fire in the moving van destroyed all the family's belongings, from the bedding to the Barbie doll, from the sweaters to the screwdrivers. Plus her desk, with all the bills and receipts she needed to substantiate the loss.

To make a claim Maureen had to recall from memory an inventory of all their possessions. "Just go through your kitchen in your mind and list the pots and pans and utensils," said Maureen with a sigh. "It's unbelievable! And then do that for every other room in your home."

Painstakingly, Maureen was able to reconstruct a loss of $40,000, but she still only received the $10,000 limit from the moving company because she hadn't evaluated her household goods for adequate coverage. To complete the horror story, she didn't even have homeowner's insurance because the family was in transit.

Admittedly, Maureen was the victim of a freak disaster, but partial loss of home furnishings is common. We have one hapless friend whose home was half destroyed in a California brushfire (at least he had homeowner's insurance), and all too many who have been robbed of silver, jewelry, and furs. Some of them were adequately insured, others weren't.

And like so many of you, we've had several all-too-ordinary accidents ourselves. Once, a leak in the upstairs bathroom ruined a sofa, some drapes, and an oriental rug. Another time, a puff-back in the furnace caused smoke damage to some old family paintings.

But at least we've never lost our luggage en route. That particular type of loss seems to be a specialty of our neighbor Tom, who loves to travel. "After the second time an airline lost my baggage," he said, "I finally took out a separate personal policy floater."

If you're a prudent property owner, you won't wait for your prize horse to bolt before you lock the barn door. Maureen, for instance, now keeps detailed lists of all her possessions. Because it's a chore most of us postpone, you'll welcome two itemized worksheets that simplify the task: *Household Inventory Record* (#47) and *Special Inventory: Record of Jewelry, Silverware, Art* (#48). Whether you own valuable antiques, furs, and jewelry, or just serviceable furniture, whether you rent or own your home, you'll find those inventories helpful if you're ever faced with a loss. They'll also help you figure out how much homeowner's insurance to buy, which we'll discuss later.

YOUR HOUSEHOLD BELONGINGS

The *Household Inventory Record* (#47) and *Special Inventory: Record of Jewelry, Silverware, Art* (#48) not only comprise a complete record of everything you own, but also give the value in case of fire or theft. It's your responsibility to prove the value of each item at the time of a loss, so make certain your property is correctly valued, and review those evaluations annually.

As you assess your property, decide whether you want to insure each item for its replacement value or for its actual cash or depreciated cost.

How to Appraise Your Household Contents

- Use the original sales receipts on major items, if you still have them.
- On brand-name goods, such as major appliances and furniture, contact department stores or retail dealers.
- For jewelry, silver, art, and antiques, get appraisals from dealers or museums.
- Contact appraisal services that will evaluate any or all of your possessions.

Since time erodes (or enhances) your possessions, we recommend that you appraise your household contents at least every three years.

If possible, complete your household inventory with a videotape or color photographs of each room so if you suffer a fire or theft, you can prove that the objects you claim actually existed. You should also take photographs of your artwork, silver, and any other valuables. Keep all tapes, photographs, and their negatives in your safe-deposit box, or in a fireproof container at home.

See if your community supports Project Theftguard or a similar program in which the police will loan you a tool to engrave your Social Security number on your valuables. It won't prevent their theft, but it may aid in their recovery.

HOMEOWNER'S INSURANCE

Homeowner's insurance will protect anything you own, from a multimillion-dollar mansion with minimal furnishings to a rented studio apartment with a Picasso painting. You don't have to own a home to need homeowner's insurance—and, indeed, that's a misconception of many renters. Whether or not you own what the insurance industry calls a dwelling, you need some form of homeowner's insurance to protect your property. You also need to know what kind to select.

Types of Homeowner's Insurance

Most homeowner's policies insure both your dwelling and your personal property. The extent of the coverage depends on how much protection you want to buy—that is, how many "perils" you want to cover. For the lowest cost you can get limited coverage under a "Basic," or "Named Perils," policy, wider coverage with a "Broad" policy, and, at the highest rates, maximum coverage under a "Comprehensive" policy, also called "all-risk" (but even the all-risk policy doesn't insure all risks, like nuclear accidents, war, and earthquakes). In addition, there are special homeowner's policies for condominium owners, as well as for renters, who only need to cover their personal property. When choosing homeowner's insurance, remember that false economy will endanger your most valuable assets.

Whatever the details and extent of individual policies, all homeowner's insurance includes the same major coverage:

- Physical damage to your property, including your dwelling and other structures on the property.
- Personal property, that is, everything in your home, insured up to a specified percentage—usually 50 percent of the value of the house. In a renter's policy, your personal property is insured at the value you designate. In all homeowner's policies there are limits on certain valuable items, such as silver, jewelry, and furs, and on away-from-home losses. Here your household inventory records (#s 47 and 48) will be helpful.
- Personal liability, normally a minimum of $100,000, in case someone has an accident on your property and sues you, plus a small medical payment for their injuries.
- Your costs of living elsewhere while your home is being repaired from fire or other insured damages.

- The loss of your personal property away from home, normally to 10 percent of the insured value of your personal property coverage.

There are other secondary provisions that can be covered in a home-owner's policy. Ask your insurance agent to recommend the individual coverage that suits your life-style.

Record the value of your home and its contents on the *Homeowner's Insurance Checklist* (#49). You'll find it will help you figure the amount of coverage you need. If you have a second home, be sure to complete a separate form for it.

Buying Property Insurance

If you're a homeowner, your most valuable property probably is your house. Be sure it's properly insured. Your insurance company normally requires you to insure your home for up to 80 percent of its total value. To induce you to "insure to value," insurance companies have a penalty clause they may invoke anytime you have a loss and you insure for less than 80 percent. Since property values are not absolute, this penalty is only applied to a claim settlement when you are dramatically underinsured.

This means that if you have a partial loss of property (and that's the most common kind), you'll be reimbursed for the full cost of repairing or replacing the loss, as long as it doesn't exceed that 80 percent figure; if you have a total loss, you'll only be reimbursed for 80 percent of the value of the house (the face amount of the policy) and you'll have to make up the difference.

If you insure for less than 80 percent of your property's total value, you'll receive proportionately less for either a partial or a complete loss.

If you want full coverage in the event of a total loss, insure your home for 100 percent of its replacement cost. "Don't think about market value of your house when you think about insurance," advises financial expert Grace W. Weinstein, author of *The Lifetime Book of Money Management.* "Replacement value, or rebuilding cost, is the key."

When you insure your home or any other item, you can insure it at its replacement value or its depreciated value (that is, actual cash value). Replacement value insurance is more expensive only because you are insuring to a higher value. However, the insurance company will pay you the cost of replacing the item at today's prices without depreciating its value. Replacement value allows you to replace an item with one of like kind and quality at today's prices. Depreciated value reimburses you for that item at today's *used* value prices. Some companies may not reimburse you until after you purchase a replacement, so you may need cash or credit to buy those items.

When You Appraise Your Home

- Don't confuse the value of your land with the value of your building; they are two separate items. The land will normally appreciate and the building will normally depreciate. This is why your real estate broker can't accurately determine the value of your home.

- Ask a contractor for the current cost per square foot of construction in your area. Multiply this cost by the square footage of your entire home and you'll have a fair idea of its replacement value.
- Get an appraisal from an appraisal service. Your insurance company or agent, or your bank, can recommend local appraisal services. Many insurance companies will estimate the insurable value of your home if your insurance agent requests it.
- Adjust the value of your home after every significant home improvement, and periodically for inflation and changing property values.

Some Buying Tips

- Buy coverage for replacement cost rather than depreciated or actual value cost whenever possible for both home and personal property.
- Read the policy carefully to see what is specifically *excluded*. Depending on where you live, you may want to buy additional coverage for one or more of those exclusions, which commonly include floods, mudslides, and earthquakes.
- Check how much your jewelry, furs, cash, silverware, and collections are insured for under your regular homeowner's policy. Most policies place a total limitation of $500 on the combined worth of all those valuables, plus other restrictions, such as the place of the loss. You can insure any specific items you choose at their replacement or depreciated value by adding an endorsement to your policy or buying a separate personal property floater that covers you wherever the loss occurs.
- If you don't have individually valuable items but feel that your general furnishings are worth more than the 50 percent your homeowner's policy automatically covers them for, you can increase that personal property coverage up to 70 percent of your home's stated value.
- Check your policy's coverage for "other structures." Most policies insure them for 10 percent of your home's value. If you have a pool house or guest cottage or any other separate structure you feel is worth more than that amount, increase that coverage in your policy.
- If you have a second home, be sure it's properly insured.
- Ask your agent about an automatic inflation-protection clause in your policy.
- Remember, homeowner's insurance is not like life insurance; for late payment there is no thirty-day extension beyond the expiration date. Mark the premium due date on your calendar in case your insurance company or agent fails to remind you of its renewal.
- Review your policy periodically, and—we repeat—adjust for inflation, home improvements, and changing property values.

How Much Does It Cost?

The premium for homeowner's insurance can vary widely among competing companies. Rates are based on the construction of your home, your proximity to fire-fighting equipment, the quality of your local fire department, the hazards of your geographic location (for example, high crime, heavy brush, unprotected beachfront), and, of course, your specific coverage and the amount of your deductible.

All homeowner's policies have deductibles. They are the amount of loss you're willing to cover yourself, before being reimbursed. The higher the deductible, the lower the premium. When choosing the deductible, follow these rules:

- Don't give up a lot for a little. Deductibles of $100, $250, or $500 are normally good buys because you get substantial discounts on your premiums. But a $5,000 deductible probably won't save you enough to warrant the high risk.
- Don't gamble more than you can afford to lose. A $100 deductible is manageable; a $10,000 deductible may not be.
- Play the odds. If you live in a high crime area, you're more vulnerable to household robbery than to the loss of jewelry you probably keep in your safe-deposit box.
- Comparison shop for the coverage you want, using the *Homeowner's Insurance Cost Comparison Worksheet* (#50). With your detailed listing of the value of your property and its contents on the *Homeowner's Insurance Checklist* (#49), you'll know exactly how much insurance you need, and you can compare coverage and prices from several insurance companies.

Making a Claim

If you've had property damage or a loss, promptly notify your insurance agent. Use the *Property Loss Reporting Form* (#51) for reports to your insurance agent, a record for yourself, and as a guide for a police report when necessary.

The insurance company will assign an adjuster to represent *them*—not you—in helping to determine the value of the loss. The adjuster has the authority to settle claims and hire contractors or repair services to resolve the claim.

If there is a major disagreement about the value of the loss, ask your insurance agent for help, get a bid from your own contractor, or request formal arbitration through your attorney. Arbitration will keep your legal costs at a minimum.

In some parts of the country (normally metropolitan areas), you can hire your own independent adjuster to represent *you*—not the insurance company—in settling the claim. Their fees are based on a percentage of your settlement. Look in the classified directory under "Public Adjuster" to see if one is in your area.

Note: Most insurance companies will pay for the cost of emergency repairs, such as boarding up broken windows and removing debris, to protect your property from further damage.

LIABILITY INSURANCE

Who hasn't had a sinking feeling when we inadvertently injure someone? Especially when it's a neighbor whose proximity reminds us daily of the deed. We know just how our friend Marylou felt as she told us about a problem with her next-door neighbor.

"Ricky fell off his bike and ruined some specimen plants that our neighbor particularly prized. And when she came over to complain, she tripped on our garden hose and broke her foot." Marylou rolled her eyes heavenward. "It was like a black comedy of errors, especially when we offered to pay for the damage—and got bills for hundreds of dollars!"

Marylou was furious at Ricky, even though it wasn't his fault. She was furious at the neighbor, though it wasn't her fault. She didn't start to smile until she found out that her homeowner's insurance covered most of the property damage and all of the personal injury claim.

As Marylou happily discovered, all homeowner's policies include liability insurance that protects you from claims or suits brought by others contending your negligence caused them harm or loss. This type of insurance commonly covers up to $100,000 for each person for bodily injury or property damage. It also pays small amounts for medical care (without having to prove negligence) to people who are injured on your premises and to reimburse others for damage you do to their property (without having to prove liability). Don't confuse this with the liability insurance included in your automobile policy; that only applies to accidents involving your car (see Chapter 15, Auto Protection).

In today's world, your homeowner's insurance may not be enough to protect you. People are more litigious than they used to be, perhaps because awards for personal injury lawsuits are increasingly substantial, often far higher than the $100,000 coverage provided by your insurance. Consider increasing your liability coverage, either under your homeowner's policy or through a separate Umbrella Liability Policy, if any of the following apply:

- You have extensive assets or a high income that might attract a personal injury suit.
- You have active young children whose athletic activities may threaten neighboring property.
- You need higher limits on your auto insurance coverage.
- You might be sued for libel, slander, or defamation of character.
- You serve on school boards, church boards, or other nonprofit organizations that don't carry insurance for their members.
- You engage in activities such as skiing and hunting where you might injure someone else.

Making a Claim

As soon as anyone in your family is involved in an accident, contact your insurance agent and complete the *Accident Reporting Form* (#52). Fill it in as soon as possible, while the details of the accident are still fresh in your mind.

Your agent will tell you if you need to make a police report and, if necessary, will have an insurance company adjuster contact you concerning a potential claim. Even though a claim may not officially be filed against you, it's a good idea to inform your agent if you think someone is considering suing you.

You may also want to give a copy of the completed *Accident Reporting Form* (#52) to your insurance agent, the insurance company's adjuster, and/ or the police. If any of them want you to complete their own forms later, use this one as the source for all pertinent information.

AUTO PROTECTION

15

In most families, the husband usually stakes out the car as his domain. He buys it, babies it, and has a special affection for it. Perhaps that's why so many women feel ill at ease whenever they have trouble on the road.

Our friend Margaret recently had a typical experience. "I was stopped at a signal, completely stopped, and a car hit me from behind," she told us. "I couldn't believe it! But even being totally in the right and knowing I had insurance, I was still confused. I didn't know what to do, whom to call, or how to handle it."

We assured Margaret she was in good company. That kind of accident happens all too frequently and, like Margaret, many of us get flustered and can't remember exactly what we're supposed to do.

As it happened, Margaret took the right first step; she motioned the other driver to the curb and asked for his driver's license—only to find the car wasn't his and it wasn't insured. "I didn't know what else to ask. I was afraid I wasn't even protected against an uninsured driver, and that the insurance company would cancel my policy."

Harriet, a young mother who lives near us, told us about a particularly traumatic incident. One day she drove her two youngsters to an ice-cream parlor. As she opened the front door to get out of her parked car and let her two children out of the backseat, a tractor truck barreled by, accordion-pleated the door, and raced on.

"It wasn't until later that I realized we were all almost killed, and I couldn't stop shaking," she said. "At the time I didn't know anything except the kids were all right. I didn't know if I could move my car. I didn't know whether to call the insurance company first or call a tow truck. And I didn't know whether I was even covered for a vehicle that doesn't stop."

Margaret and Harriet were lucky because no one was injured in their accidents. Even so, they came up against two potentially serious situations: an uninsured driver, and a hit-and-run accident. But even if you just skid into the next car, you'd be wise to know if your policy is adequate.

Ignorance about automobile insurance is probably more common than fender benders on a slick road. If you have an accident, do you know what to do? Do you understand your automobile insurance? Do you know exactly what—and who—it will cover, and to what extent? Do you have enough protection? You'll really be in the driver's seat when you're savvy about your car insurance.

CAR INSURANCE

Usually, all automobile insurance includes the same basic elements:

Bodily injury liability.   This protects you against claims for medical expenses and legal judgments resulting from injury or death to passengers in your car, to pedestrians, and to people in other cars when you are at fault. Family policies cover *anyone* driving your car with your permission, and all your family members who drive someone else's car with that owner's permission. ("Family members" can be over age eighteen as long as their primary residence is with you, even though they are away at school.) This is the single most important element in car insurance because it shields you from potential economic disaster resulting from accident claims.

Note: Auto insurance liability rests with the registered owner. If you continue to keep your college students' cars registered in your name, you are assuming responsibility for a liability claim.

Basic (not family) auto policies are more limited because they cover only persons named on the policy and only while driving your car.

This coverage is usually written with one limit for injury to any one person, and one maximum limit for any one accident.

Property damage liability.   This pays for damage to another person's property when you are at fault. Like bodily injury liability, it covers anyone driving your car with your permission, and all members of your family who drive another car with the owner's permission.

The limit for property damage is separate from bodily injury.

No-fault auto liability.   In those states in which it is available, your own liability insurance will cover you no matter who is at fault. You are protected for bodily injury, including medical expenses and any loss of income.

Uninsured or underinsured motorist coverage.   This protects you against claims for bodily injuries caused by a hit-and-run driver, by an uninsured driver, and by an underinsured driver whose policy doesn't cover all your expenses. This coverage applies to each person in the car, but has a maximum total limit for the accident. It also covers any family members riding in someone else's car or injured as pedestrians.

Medical payments coverage. This pays medical expenses for you or your passengers in an accident, no matter who was at fault. It, too, covers everyone in your car and all family members riding in anyone else's car or struck by a car while walking. This differs from bodily injury liability because you collect from your own company without having to prove the other party negligent.

Collision coverage. You are reimbursed, without regard to fault, for damage to your car caused in a collision with another car, with any other stationary object, or if your car overturns. It always has a deductible that you must pay. If the other driver is at fault, your insurance company will try to collect the deductible from that driver.

Comprehensive insurance. This pays you for other damages to your car, such as theft, fire, flood, wind, vandalism, and window breakage, without regard to fault. Usually there is a deductible on each loss.

Certain items, such as car telephones, CB radios, and stereos, are covered only if they are permanently installed in your automobile.

Normally you will be insured for the actual cash value of your car and/ or its parts, and not for the replacement value. The insurance company will offer you the "used value" of your car if you have a total loss, and will depreciate any partial repairs. For example, if your car's engine is damaged in an accident, you might not be reimbursed for the full cost of a new engine.

If you disagree with the settlement your insurance company offers, you have the right to sue or request arbitration.

Accidental death and dismemberment. This covers all passengers in your car up to a certain limit, and includes permanent disability. This is not a standard clause, but you can add it to most policies for an additional premium.

Car Insurance Rates

The cost of automobile insurance varies widely because different companies base their rates on different factors. These include your geographic area; the age, sex, and driving records of the drivers; how the car is used; and even the age and cost of the car. An urban male driver under twenty-five clocking 20,000 miles a year on business will pay higher premiums than a suburban married woman who drives 10,000 miles for marketing and car pooling.

Buying Tips

- Get insurance prices from more than one company; compare their methods of adjusting claims as well as their rates and coverage. For example, some companies allow you to select your repair garage, others require you to bring your car to them for inspection.
- Don't skimp on bodily injury liability. Always buy high limits, $1 million if available.

- Consider increasing the property damage liability in your basic policy. Many people carry high bodily injury limits but not enough property damage liability, not realizing, for example, that if they hit a building and caused a fire or explosion, the property damage would exceed their coverage.
- Get higher limits of uninsured and underinsured motorist coverage. Despite the insurance requirements in most states, many drivers are not adequately covered, so it's prudent to provide your own protection.
- Consider towing and rental car coverage. The premium is small and the potential savings great if you have to rent a car for a week or two while your own car is disabled by a covered loss.
- Check these seven ways to reduce your insurance costs but not your coverage:

1. Take advantage of safe driver discounts. Consider isolating the good drivers in your family on one policy, and the poor drivers on another policy. You might even put your teenage sons under a state-assigned risk plan (if your state has one) to protect your "good driver" discounts.
2. Notify your insurance company if you drive less, or no longer drive to and from work.
3. Check for "good student" or driver education discounts.
4. Look for additional discounts for car pools, for nonsmoking, nondrinking senior citizens, or for insuring more than one car with the same company.
5. Consider rewriting your policy if the company rated you on the number of driving tickets you received in the preceding thirty-six months, and if, before the midterm point in the policy, you no longer have three tickets in the preceding thirty-six months. For example, in January say you had three tickets in the past thirty-six months, but by May you only had one ticket in the preceding thirty-six months. By rewriting your policy at the six-month midpoint, you can substantially reduce your premium for the balance of the year.
6. Take higher deductibles on collision and comprehensive insurance. The deductible is the amount you pay toward a loss before your insurance takes over.
7. Consider dropping collision insurance when your car is four or five years old and would cost more to repair than it's worth.

Whenever you buy car insurance, review the *Automobile Insurance Checklist (#53)* in the Workbook section at the end of the book, and use the *Insurance Premium Cost Comparison (#54)* when you get competitive quotes.

WHEN YOU HAVE AN ACCIDENT

In the Workbook section you'll find an *Automobile Accident Reporting Form (#55)* to help you compile the facts your insurance company will want to know about any accident involving you or your car. You may want to keep these in your car's glove compartment.

If you have an accident, follow these steps:

1. Before leaving the scene, give your name, address, and driver's license to those involved, and to a police officer if you can find one.
2. Write down the names, drivers' licenses, and insurance companies of all people involved. Also, get the names, addresses, and telephone numbers of any witnesses to the accident. Record everything on the *Automobile Accident Reporting Form (#55)*.
3. Note the make, year, and license plate of other cars involved; any property that was damaged; passengers who appear to be injured; and be able to describe the circumstances and site of the accident. As soon as possible, write this information on the *Automobile Accident Reporting Form (#55)*.
4. If a driver refuses to give you the information, or drives off without stopping, try to note as much information as you can: the license plate, color, make, and year of the vehicle, and any commercial lettering on it.
5. Don't express an opinion about who was at fault, and don't talk about the accident or give any statement to anyone except the police.
6. Report the accident immediately to your insurance company or agent, even if the claim appears to be minor. There is always the danger that someone might later claim injury and blame you. Failure to notify your insurance company can void your insurance coverage.

Tips for Dealing with an Insurance Adjuster

- Remember that insurance adjusters, whether they are on staff or hired as outside adjusters or inspectors, represent the insurance company, not you.
- If an adjuster doesn't look at your car within seven working days, contact your insurance company again.
- Review the repair shop's estimated bill, including the use of new or used parts. Be sure the repair is being done to your specifications; once you sign the insurance release, you have no further claim against the company.
- If you have any questions or doubts, call your insurance agent or a supervisor at the insurance company.
- If you have a serious disagreement with the other insurance company, consult a lawyer and consider arbitration to resolve the problem.

V

HITTING YOUR STRIDE IN SPITE OF A TRAGEDY

WHEN A DEATH OCCURS

16

"As I was driving to the hospital, I didn't really want to think about what I felt—I felt he wasn't going to be all right at all," said Carol. "And when the doctor came into the waiting room, I knew. The paramedics had never gotten a heartbeat on him."

Carol, a young Chicago mother, has relived that day many times since Bud's fatal heart attack in his office. It is a memory laced with many emotions—disbelief, shock, grief, even irony. Just the evening before, they had taken their twelve-year-old daughter shopping for her coming birthday.

"We sat in the mall and watched her, and talked about how great she was and what a joy it was to see her grow." Even after two years, it's still hard for Carol to talk about that day. "It was terrible," she says softly. "Words can't describe it."

Carol was caught totally off guard by the call from Bud's secretary, but even if you have warning, is a wife ever prepared for the shock of her husband's death? Sally is a woman in New York whose husband had Hodgkin's disease for ten years. "It went on for so long that I began to think everything would be all right," she said, "and then Peter's health started to fail and it was touch and go for the last two years. When he finally died, I couldn't believe it."

You can expect a seriously ill person to die, yet still not anticipate the shock of that loss. An unexpected death, like Bud's, simply stuns the mind and body. You're unprepared to deal with it either emotionally or logically.

Emotional recovery takes hard work and time. But unfortunately, the legal and financial demands of a death don't leave us enough time to regain a clear-thinking mind or a logical perspective. Just at this moment of crisis you—the survivor—must make dozens of difficult, critical decisions about your family's business and future.

Because too many mistakes are made during this traumatic period, you'll find a *Transition Plan Checklist* (#56) in the Workbook section of this book to guide you through the first difficult months. We have expanded a chronology in *The Widow's Guide to Life*, by Ida Fisher and Byron Lane, (Lane Con Press, 1985) to provide a checklist of the various details you should discharge after a death, many of them legally required. By lifting the burden of finding out what to do, this checklist allows you to act almost automatically.

Carol remembered the first days after Bud died. "I was numb and in a state of shock, which I guess was fortunate. You can function fine in shock. I would just concentrate on whatever I had to do." With the *Transition Plan Checklist* (#56) in hand, you'll know exactly what you have to do, and when.

You'll also learn what you don't have to do. "You'll be besieged with advice from relatives, friends, and your husband's associates," said Julie, the family counselor who has been a widow for seven years. "You know: move out of your house right away; sell the second car; talk to my wonderful money manager who can invest your life insurance money." When you know what must be done, you'll also know what can be deferred. Understanding that there are decisions you can postpone can relieve some of the stress, because all the women we met—widows and divorcées both—agreed that the worst time to make a decision is right after a traumatic event.

As you review the Transition Plan below, you'll see there are many tedious tasks. Don't be discouraged. They do take time. You may want to follow Carol's example. "Even with the good accountants, attorneys, and other people who helped me, it took a lot of time to collect information and get the right documents to the right people," she said. "I decided to take one year off and get all the paperwork done, before finding a job."

THE TRANSITION PLAN

Whether you track down the information and file the necessary papers yourself, or you delegate tasks to other people, make it your responsibility to keep the *Transition Plan Checklist* (#56) up to date. It's your best way of being sure that important documents are filed and decisions are made within the necessary time.

As you can see from the chronology, some decisions must be made at once, others can wait for six to nine months or longer. Within each time period, they are listed in order of decreasing urgency.

At Once

1. Make funeral arrangements. If you are one of the few couples who have already made funeral plans, you'll be grateful for that guidance. Most people are like Sally. "There was a lot of planning in those last months of Peter's illness," she said, "but the one thing I could never bring myself to discuss was the funeral. Peter tried to talk about it once. 'Don't waste money on a funeral,' he said. In the end, I muddled through by myself."

2. Decide on obituary notices. You may not want to notify your local newspapers if you have small children or a large estate, and particularly if your husband's death is not unexpected; you will avoid calls from salesmen and other people at a difficult time. However, you may want to send a notice to former hometown papers, school alumni associations, and other professional organizations.

3. Notify relatives.

4. Notify friends or, better yet, ask close friends to help you with this difficult task.

5. Open a checking account in your own name, if you don't already have one.

Within the First 30 Days

1. Get at least twenty *certified* copies of the death certificate. You'll need to produce them for many reasons, such as collecting life insurance claims, transferring title or ownership of properties, cars, etc. In most cases, the funeral home can get the copies for you.

2. Put all joint checking and savings accounts in your name, and keep those accounts separate from any probate proceedings. Your bank will probably request that you maintain a reserve in the old account for any checks that may be outstanding.

3. Establish a new "estate" bank account in the name of the deceased for the checks that will come in, such as life insurance proceeds. The funds can probably not be used until probate is completed, but at least they will draw interest in a safe account. After probate, these funds will pay the estate's bills.

4. Notify all insurance companies, and start to file for benefits.

5. Review the auto insurance policy. It may carry medical or accidental death and dismemberment coverage in addition to the life insurance benefits.

6. Check your medical insurance policies immediately for any time limitations for filing claims for benefits. Also check the benefits themselves to see if additional coverage, such as accidental death, can be claimed. Ask your insurance agent to do this for you.

7. If the death was accidental and occurred while traveling, notify all the credit card companies; many of them automatically include travel accident insurance as part of their services.

8. Report the death to the local Social Security Administration office, and ask them to send you its guide on Social Security benefits. Social Security benefits are not automatic.

9. Apply for Social Security benefits. You must appear personally with the following documents in hand: a copy of the death certificate, your husband's and your Social Security numbers, a copy of your marriage certificate to him, a copy of your birth certificate, copies of birth certificates of all children under age eighteen (even if they are from former marriages), and verification of your husband's earnings (you can use your husband's last income tax return).

10. If your husband was a veteran, contact the Veteran's Administra-

tion for benefits. Some states have their own veteran's benefits. Both the federal and state governments will want the same information you furnished the Social Security Administration, plus a copy of his discharge papers. If you can't locate them, write to the National Personnel Records Center, Military Personnel Records, 9700 Page Boulevard, St. Louis, MO 63132.

11. Notify your husband's employer or associates, but don't assume they will automatically file for the benefits that are due you. Make a friend of someone in the office to help you; normally the personnel department has someone skilled in this area.

12. If your husband's death was work-related, file for Workers Compensation benefits. You would make a claim through your husband's employer, who would file it with its Workers Compensation insurance company.

13. Check all places where your husband could have purchased life insurance: clubs, fraternal, professional, or charitable organizations, school alumni associations, credit life insurance on loans, or travel life insurance through credit cards.

14. Have your broker transfer all securities to your name as soon as possible. By transferring title, you will acquire a source of ready cash, if needed. If your securities were held in joint tenancy, they will not have to go through probate.

15. If you have U.S. Savings Bonds in joint tenancy, you can either have the bank reissue them in your name or cash them in at once. They won't have to go through probate.

16. Your safe-deposit box, which in most states is sealed after a death, can be opened under certain circumstances. If you furnish a certified copy of the death certificate, you can look for a will, burial instructions, or life insurance policies.

If some of the contents of the box are your separate property, you have the right to remove them so they are not included in the estate. The bank may require proof of your ownership, such as a bill of sale.

Get another safe-deposit box so you can protect your valuables in the interim while the family box is sealed, which will be until probate is completed.

17. Notify all IRA and Keogh accounts. The manner in which the account was set up will determine how its funds are distributed.

18. If you are short of funds, refer to Chapter 5, Borrowing, and the *Emergency Disability Plan* (#45) for ways to find ready cash.

19. Look for assets in the income tax records. For example, Schedule B lists interest and dividend income, and names each stock, mutual fund, and taxable bond that generated income. If you don't have a copy of the return, get one from your accountant or regional office of the Internal Revenue Service.

Within the Next 60 Days

1. Select an estate attorney to represent your interests and to file your husband's will. Your husband's attorney may not specialize in estates, and

he may have a conflict of interest if he also represents your husband's business. See Chapter 2, Picking Your Advisory Team, for help in finding an attorney.

2. Pick an accountant to handle the financial transactions that will occur during this period. He must file federal estate and inheritance tax returns. Work closely with him on those transactions. Again, your husband's accountant may have a conflict of interest that will force you to select a new advisor.

3. Transfer title on your home and any other real estate that you owned jointly to your own name.

4. Transfer title on the cars. The way in which title was jointly held and how the estate is being settled will govern how the transfer may be made. If the bank holds title to your car, the bank's loan officer will help you with the transfer.

5. Notify your insurance agent to change the auto and homeowner's policies to your name.

6. Cancel and change all credit cards to your name. To protect your credit, make sure you pay all bills promptly. If you don't feel ready for that yet, ask your accountant to pay them for you for a time.

7. Change all the utilities to your name.

8. Change the listing in the telephone directory; for personal security use only your first initial, not your first name.

9. If your husband was a beneficiary on your life insurance policies, notify your life insurance agent to remove his name.

10. Review your own medical insurance to be sure it is adequate.

11. Revise your will to reflect your current situation and desires.

12. Notify all creditors of your situation.

13. Select a financial advisor to counsel you on your investments (you may be receiving large sums of money from life insurance benefits), but try to postpone any major decisions you don't feel up to making and be conservative in those you do. If possible, pick an advisor who only counsels, not sells.

Within the Next 6 Months

1. Work up a new budget for the means you now have on hand. Use the worksheets in Chapter 7, Budgeting.

2. Review your life insurance needs to be sure you are including all the beneficiaries you want to, and that you are protecting the estate adequately.

3. Update your will.

4. Since you will have revised much of your financial information since the death of your husband, record this new financial data on appropriate worksheets in the Workbook section so it's up to date for your heirs if anything happens to you. Review all the worksheets in light of your new status, especially #s 1 to 11, which are explained in Chapter 1, Keeping Family Records and Documents.

5. Review the *Disability Insurance Checklist* (#44) to see if you are adequately protected.

6. Consult with your financial advisor about starting your investment plan so that all your assets are protected.

7. Take time to review all your records going back at least two years—check stubs, bank statements, and business correspondence—to search for additional life insurance coverage and other assets you didn't know existed.

8. Review the *Checklist of Executor's Duties* (#57) and make certain the executor is doing his job.

USING YOUR SURVIVAL INSTINCTS 17

"One day you have a new feeling about yourself," said Vicki, a real estate agent in Los Angeles who was widowed three years ago. "You think: I'm a survivor. I know I can handle it. I might not like what's going on. I may get upset. Sometimes I still feel hurt and angry, but I know I'm going to make it."

Vicki's newfound sense of self at age forty-three didn't come easy, but it did come. "The hardest part—aside from the loneliness and missing Fred in so many ways, especially since we worked together—was the scary realization there's only me." Who else would take Freddie to Little League? Who else would clean the garage? Who in the household would even enjoy a French movie on the weekend? Was her foreseeable restaurant future inescapably wedded to fast food? How often would their friends invite a fifth wheel to dinner?

During these last years alone, it seemed to Vicki that her world divided into two parts: the obligations she had to take over from Fred, and the fun she feared she would never know again. "I felt so empty," she said. "I realize now I didn't have a separate life of my own that could go on independently."

Women of Vicki's vintage, wives who grew up just ahead of the women's movement, frequently rely on their families for their identity, their emotional needs, even their friends. For many of them, having a job was independence enough; spending separate time with one's own friends or colleagues seemed disloyal to their husbands.

Finding a sense of self takes initiative, planning, and sometimes courage to invest in what twice-widowed Ida Fisher calls "survival insurance." But universally, widows have told us that it's critical to a woman's recovery, and very few women carry it.

"Women regard life insurance and health insurance as good investments," says Shelli Chosak, a Los Angeles therapist who counsels widows and is herself a widow. "But they don't want to think about emotional insurance to help develop internal strengths and build a sense of identity, purpose, and personal power."

It's important that you consciously begin to develop resources for yourself that you can use now or call on later. So many of the women we interviewed wished they had developed a support system for themselves *before* they were traumatized by widowhood or divorce.

Family counselors also observe that the women who recover fastest are the ones who have independent lives and identities of their own. "I was lucky because I always led the life of an individual," said Vicki. "I never lived through my husband. I never lived through my children. But I know other women who only saw themselves as Mrs. Somebody, without an identity of their own. They were devastated."

SURVIVAL INSURANCE—INVESTING IN YOURSELF

How can wives develop emotional resources that they can use now or call on later? Women who have been widowed or divorced, and counselors who work with them, suggest a number of ways.

Enlist Your Husband's Support

Many a woman sees developing her own identity as a threat to her marriage, and it can be. Very often the first step to a more self-sufficient life is to share your need for it with your husband. By enlisting his support you reassure him, gain an ally, and start to free yourself from feeling dependent and guilty. Moreover, you'll have the companionship, advice, and assistance of somebody who really cares about you.

Swap Household Responsibilities

Many wives leave certain household chores to their husbands—repairs, maintenance, paying the monthly bills, as well as more complex financial matters—and they have problems when they find themselves alone. Marybeth, a young widow in Minneapolis, counts herself lucky that she wasn't one of them. "My husband was a busy doctor, and he didn't have time to look after the house. If we needed a new roof, repairs, whatever, he didn't want to hear about it. He just wanted me to take care of it. After he died and there was a leaky faucet or the boat needed a new motor, it was easy for me to get estimates and make a decision. It was particularly helpful that I was in charge all along."

As you take on so-called masculine chores, encourage your husband to become similarly self-sufficient. "I tell men's groups that it's just as important for them to know how to cook a meal, do the laundry, and clean the house as it is for their wives to balance the checkbook and make investments," says Ida Fisher, who counsels bereaved women and men. "We should all be prepared to do everything for ourselves."

Expand and Enrich Your Social Circle

Start now to develop new relationships and friendships that please just you. Enlarge your circle, seek new friends, even single friends. Open yourself to all kinds of people—older, younger, men, women, even children. Find ways to enrich your existing friendships so they will weather the loss of your husband. "When you lose a husband, your married friends often feel uncomfortable with you, or you feel uncomfortable with them, and the relationship starts to dissipate," warns Vicki.

To guard against that reality, build your single network while you are still part of a couple. You'll find you're not only protecting your future, you're enriching your present.

Find New Interests and Nurture Old Ones

For anyone trying to find an independent way, either for future careers or present pleasures, there is no right place to start—as long as you start. Reach out and take advantage of everything. Experiment. Research. Test. Try unfamiliar terrain. If you're a wonderful cook, resist a cooking class for something unfamiliar that piques your interest, say, archeology. If you enjoy politics, join a study/action group such as the League of Women Voters. If you like helping people, participate in a volunteer service organization. You'll not only tap wellsprings of satisfaction, you'll be forming those important new friendships.

If you're altogether stymied, try to revitalize your early dreams and ambitions. Try to reconnect with your feelings and interests before you were married. Recall your favorite games and hobbies as a youngster. All these give clues to dormant interests.

For ideas on how to identify interests and generate ideas, turn to the following chapter, The Job Market, even if you're not thinking of working.

Second Wind—Rebuilding and Growing

Because the death of a husband is so tragic, it's ironic that so many positive things can result if a woman is open to the possibilities. We must believe and accept that we can go through traumatic experiences that would ordinarily crush us, and not only emerge whole, but perhaps more complete. We all have the power to create wonderful and meaningful lives for ourselves.

Making new friends, testing new interests, trying on a new self-sufficient persona, often take courage. It's frightening to go out and put yourself on the line when you are living in a safe and protected environment. It is much more terrifying when you're widowed or divorced.

It may help to know that when Shelli Chosak counsels widows and divorcées, she crystallizes the challenge by describing the Chinese symbol for crisis, which is made up of two words: danger and opportunity. "To the

Chinese, when people face a crisis, it's like arriving at a fork in a road," she says. "You can choose the danger road, or the opportunity road. A crisis often forces you to do things you've never done before." It's an opportunity to discover parts of yourself that have lain dormant. To discover resources you never knew you had. To learn that there are many things you can do for yourself.

That's what happened to Vicki. Several months after Fred's fatal heart attack, she planned a week-long car trip with the children, her first without him. "It was one of the scariest things I ever did," she said, "but I always wanted to go to Big Sur and I wasn't going to let my life stop because my husband died."

Vicki tried to plan for every contingency. She outlined her route in detail. She confirmed and reconfirmed her motel reservations. She left nothing to chance. She returned beaming. "I found out it was much easier than I expected, and I was so proud of myself for going."

THE DIVIDENDS OF SURVIVAL INSURANCE

To count the blessings of being self-sufficient is like acknowledging that it's nice to be accomplished, thin, and rich. But the joy of feeling independent, especially when you don't have to be, is astonishing to most women. Even the simplest things are liberating. Take Janet, the office manager of a Houston law firm, when she made her first solo business trip. Janet felt the same heart-soaring accomplishment as Vicki—and she was returning to her husband the next day.

It was clear from Vicki and Janet, and so many others we met, that what a woman does on her own, anything she hasn't done before, makes her feel better about herself. She feels in charge of her life. It doesn't matter how big or small it is; all that matters is that it means something to her.

Contrary to their apprehensions, wives who explore new horizons enhance a marriage rather than threaten it. Marriages become richer when women (and men) are more interesting. A nice turnabout of spousal admiration occurred recently at a family conference in California when one middle-aged husband confided to the audience the story of his late-blooming wife: "My wife has been married once, but I've been married three times—all to the same woman. I've had three different women in my life, and it's been fascinating to get to know all the people who exist in her."

For every woman, independence and growth are more than personal triumphs. Self-sufficiency and inner strength are the keys to survival, and to a sense of personal power.

THE JOB MARKET *18*

What do I have to offer?

Who would want me after so many years at home?

Am I good enough? Can I compete?

Where do I start?

How much can I earn?

Who'll take care of the children?

These were some of the troubled questions we heard as we interviewed women—married, widowed, and divorced—who were thinking of going, or returning, to work. Lack of confidence in their skills and lack of knowledge of the workplace was universal. Their feelings of inadequacy are understandable—and largely undeserved.

A suburban New Yorker named Mary could speak for many of the women we met. Mary has a lively interest in finance, and before she was married she worked for an investment house as an assistant to an account executive. After she and Jeff married and had twins, she fell into a host of volunteer activities. "I never could say no. I raised money for the historical society, baked for the church sales, lobbied for PTA educational funding issues in the state capital, and spent three years on the school board."

Then Jeff had a heart attack. Mary quit everything. Once Jeff was fully recovered, Mary no longer wanted to do volunteer work. She wanted paid work. "I need to feel I can take care of myself if anything happens to Jeff," she said. "That's very important to me." Mary hesitated, and her pause underlined the two unspoken questions: What? How?

There are no easy answers to the fears of most women who contemplate work for the first time or after a lengthy leave of absence. And underlying all these anxieties is the first major hurdle you have to face: fear of failure and the possibility of rejection. Only you can convince yourself that you have something to contribute, and that you can succeed.

You can be sure of certain things. First, it's not likely that someone will call you with the ideal position. You will have to do your best to make it happen.

Second, it will take a great deal of effort.

Third, you must prepare yourself for the challenge. The better prepared you are, the better your chances for success.

FIRST STEPS TO A JOB

There are many books on job seeking. Our purpose is to recap the good advice widely available elsewhere, and present it with worksheets that can clarify your efforts at every step.

Start off by treating your job search as a job in itself. Establish working hours, and stick to them. Set daily goals: the number of contacts you'll call or letters you'll write. Allocate time to polish your résumé and your interview skills.

Then turn to the two important questions: What can you do? What would you like to do? Too often most of us follow the "ready-fire-aim" philosophy of acting first and thinking later.

What Can You Do?

Obviously, the better you can evaluate your skills, the easier your job search will be. You may be aware of many of your strengths, but you may be surprised at strong points you don't know you have. Read Richard Bolles's *What Color Is Your Parachute?* for its excellent section on identifying, evaluating, and ranking your skills, plus lists of careers that utilize your skills. Review its multipage listing and identify those you do well.

Then turn to Shirley Sloan Fader's *From Kitchen to Career*, which shows how to translate your volunteer and household skills—management, fundraising, public relations, public speaking, personnel—into interesting paid work.

If you need help, many local colleges have testing and placement centers where you can evaluate your skills, and vocational and planning classes to help you channel them.

What Would You Like to Do?

Once you have some feeling for what you do best, pick a place where you can relax, sit down with the *Job-Skills Worksheet* (#58) in the Workbook section of this book, and dream up all the jobs you'd like to have. Place them in no particular order. Don't feel limited by what you're doing now, or what you have done. List everything; qualify nothing. Compile your "wish list" by free associating. If ideas don't flow easily, read newspaper ads to prime the pump.

When we urged Mary to try the worksheet, she hesitantly began to jot down a few ideas, some wilder than others:

mountain-climbing guide
space pilot
the boss of anything with a corner office and a secretary
Paris restaurant critic
any job with no morning hours

Then she listed some of the accomplishments she was proudest of:

her fluent French
organizing the town's Independence Day fair
getting the senator to speak at the fair
introducing the senator before 10,000 people
her ability to get along with people

As Mary continued to write down both silly and serious jobs in one column, and all her major and minor triumphs in the other, she began to see connections. She saw she was good at organizing events and solving problems. Could she become an administrative assistant to an executive? (It might even give her a corner office and her own secretary.) She saw she could couple her French with her interest in people. What about translating? She could speak in public. Was promotion or sales work up her alley? After she threw in her knowledge of the city, and saw she'd be an ideal resource for resident international personnel and visiting dignitaries, she started thinking of offering her services to the United Nations or another international agency.

When you have completed your own *Job-Skills Worksheet* (#58), let it sit for a few days. Now begin to eliminate those jobs that are clearly not practical (Himalayan guide, astronaut). But only remove those that are truly far-out; sometimes what appears impractical can become a reality.

Then review your *Job-Skills Worksheet* (#58) with a creative eye; try to match your interests with your expertise and experience. You're likely to be surprised. We tried this worksheet out on a group of women and saw them make some wonderful connections. One woman, for instance, who felt her enthusiasm for people and cooking could only lead her to chair the church bake-off, saw she could be a demonstrator and spokesperson for a food processor manufacturer. Another woman recognized that years of keeping her husband's books (as a volunteer) eminently qualified her as a professional bookkeeper.

A third was fascinated with oral history, but she spent several days a week doing something far different—visiting the elderly as a community volunteer. As she listened to their nostalgic stories, she realized she was being perfectly trained to start her own oral history service.

Creative job matches abounded in our group, and several people launched their own businesses, virtually overnight it seemed. One young wife who loved shopping started a shopping service for corporate executives. Another began to value her green thumb and now provides plants for corporate offices. Two others are antiques freaks; they use their expertise as appraisers.

What Do You Need to Earn?

Coupled with the search for your ideal job must be the practical assessment of how much you need to earn and how much these jobs will pay. A review of Chapter 7, Budgeting, will help you focus your financial needs.

Your State Employment Office and the U.S. Department of Labor can give you statistics on salary ranges for specific work in your area.

Your own financial (and emotional) status will dictate how quickly you want to work. If you're pressesd for money, you may not have the luxury of waiting for your ideal position. But while you're earning money, you can continue the search for the job you really want.

ROADS TO THE JOB MARKET

Even when you know what you want to do and are confident you can do it, how do you find the opportunity? Tracking down jobs takes diligence and perseverence. Here are some productive techniques.

Networking. This is the use of contacts to introduce you to favorable situations. Occasionally networking puts you in a job, but more often it directs you to other people who can give you advice, open doors, help you on your way.

There are two types of networking: casual and formal. Casual networking occurs, for example, at a cocktail party where you exchange ideas and experiences with someone, building a rapport without design. Casual networking can lay the foundation for future contact, but your gains are largely arbitrary and lack the intensity of formal networking.

In formal networking you identify the contacts who may be able to assist you with your career change. You make a deliberate effort to list those individuals, contact them, follow up on their leads and advice, and keep in continued touch with them. The *Formal Networking Record* (#59) and the *Casual Networking Record* (#60) in the Workbook section will help you keep track of all your contacts.

Mentor relationships. These are similar to conscious networking. To find a mentor, seek people who are successful in the career field that interests you. Most accomplished professionals are gratified to share their experience, guidance, and advice.

Other sources. Some places for job leads include college placement offices, private employment agencies, church registers, and local unemployment offices.

Temporary help agencies.   These are good stopgap places at which to work, particularly if you're still unsure of what you want to do and if you need to find employment quickly. They will introduce you to a variety of jobs, develop your own skills and experience, and increase your confidence. Moreover, they give prospective employers a chance to see you in action. But work for a temporary help agency only if, and as long as, you can test job fields and hone skills.

Unpaid professional work.   This is another way to explore the job market. Volunteer to work for a friend or within a particular industry at no pay. Your primary purpose is to learn the field, a particular job, or certain skills, but you may find that if you do your work well, you'll eventually be offered a permanent position.

Newspaper employment ads.   These are good guides to the current job market. Study your local newspaper to see who's hiring for what types of positions. Sometimes these ads give salary ranges. If you only see one ad for a position, you can assume it isn't a job category with wide opportunities.

You should not only answer the interesting ads, you should also consider placing one yourself if you feel you have a saleable skill.

Your main purpose in answering an ad is to get an interview with the employer. Whether you respond by letter or telephone, give only enough information to qualify you for the interview; omit details that will screen you out immediately.

Employment agencies.   These fall into three categories, depending on how they are paid:

1.   You pay a fee up-front and the agency keeps the fee even if it doesn't find you a job. Before using this type of agency, investigate it carefully; many are not legitimate.
2.   You pay the fee if the agency finds you an acceptable job. Some agencies put a time limit on their searches, and may require a nonreturnable fee thereafter, even if their search is unsuccessful.
3.   The employer pays the fee. This normally is a percentage of your annual salary, and it is returned to the employer if you don't stay in your job for thirty days. Obviously this is the best arrangement for you.

Employment agencies have a high turnover of personnel themselves, so select an agency with a good reputation, and try to work with someone who has chosen this as a career and who specializes in your field.

Before going to an agency, brush up on your skills. Generally, your typing, shorthand, word processing, and clerical skills will be tested. Be willing to investigate every position that meets your needs. And after your initial visit, keep in touch with your interviewer regularly to keep your application in the active file.

Executive search firms.   These are helpful if you are currently employed and feel you have a particularly marketable skill. Keep in mind that, unlike most employment agencies, search firms work for the employers, not the job seekers; they will only be interested in you if your work history fits a client's needs. Their prime market is highly paid executives, so they aren't a good source of employment for women re-entering the work force without unique skills and experience.

Home Work

If you can't work outside your home at the moment, there are firms that hire women to do work at home. This is a great opportunity to utilize your talents while meeting your household obligations. Moreover, many women successfully run their own businesses from home. Telephone soliciting, typing, word processing, home baby-sitting, calligraphy, music lessons, tutoring, bookkeeping, graphic design, catering, and marketing their own handicrafts are just a few enterprises that maximize home-based skills and talents.

Some women work their own hours, but not necessarily at home. Kate, a Connecticut woman who was widowed last year, lectures on color and the personality of dress. "I can structure it the way I want," she said, "and take time off when my kids have school vacation." Marybeth, the young Minneapolis widow, took a more traditional route as a real estate broker. "It was a good field for me because I'm my own boss. I work from nine to three, and I'm home for the children after school."

There are also many direct sales companies that enable you to work on a flexible schedule. Major companies include Tupperware, P.O. Box 2353, Orlando, FL 32802; Amway Corporation, 7575 East Fullton Road, Ada, MI 49355; Mary Kay Cosmetics, P.O. Box 47033, Dallas, TX 75247; and Avon Products, 9 West 57th Street, New York, NY 10019. You can get the names of additional direct sales companies at a reference library.

THE RÉSUMÉ

Whether you're trying to move into a better position, re-enter the job market, or land your first job, you'll have to write a résumé. For some reason this seems to bother many people. If you think of a résumé as merely offering an employer a clear, concise summary of your background, you may find it easier to begin.

The main thrust of your résumé is to create an interest in you. Everything else is secondary. As you compile all aspects of your background—paid and volunteer experiences, education, and personal qualifications—screen out everything that isn't germane to your job search. The fact that you play the violin in a string quartet will be an asset if you're applying for the post of development director of your local symphony, but of no interest to a bank personnel office. Apply the "so what" test to each item in your résumé. Whenever you can answer "So what!" to a statement, remove it.

You can organize your résumé in three ways: a functional résumé based on skills, a chronological résumé that tracks your job history, or a combination of the two. Study the samples of each (pages 131, 133–134, and 135–136) and choose the format that best displays your qualifications.

A *functional résumé* can turn unrelated activities into a coherent business background if your employment history is spotty or scattered, you have heavy volunteer activities, and even if you think you have nothing to offer. Moreover, by grouping your experience under descriptive skills or functions, you will mask extended absences from the conventional workplace. It also enables you to minimize any positions that don't apply to your current job search.

A *chronological résumé* will be most effective if your experience is largely in one field and you have advanced in it fairly consistently. This is the easiest to prepare because you structure it with dates and events.

A *combined functional and chronological résumé* gives you a way to display your relevant skills and still satisfy an employer's desire to see your previous employment record. Use it only if your work history is fairly solid, even though it doesn't show steady advancement or concentration in one field.

We've provided a *Résumé Worksheet* (#61) to help you organize your employment information.

Tips for Writing Your Résumé

Whichever format you choose for your résumé, keep these guidelines in mind:

- Organize the résumé on one page. An employer wants to see quickly whether you are a candidate. (This is sometimes difficult with a combined résumé.)
- Summarize your experience in concise narrative style, simple language with infrequent use of "I." Keep your paragraphs short, at most seven to ten lines.
- Describe important career-related activities other than employment, and give specifics. For fund-raising, for example, tell how you met or exceeded your goal.
- List other qualifications if they are important to the job, such as fluency in foreign languages, use of a car or computer.
- Indicate what you want in a job. It might be the challenge, the chance for advancement, or a long-term position.
- List important references only; you only need three.
- Adjust your résumé for each potential position. The same résumé is not likely to attract every employer. Use job titles and language appropriate to each position. If you are answering a want ad, use the language of the ad.
- Ask a mentor or business friends to critique your résumé before you submit it.
- Type your final copy on good quality bond paper, 8½ by 11, with a new ribbon (and no typos). To duplicate it, use a machine that makes high-quality reproductions.

How to Submit Your Résumé

Always send a cover letter with your résumé (see pages 137 and 139). Its purpose is to get the reader's attention, to identify you, and to distinguish you from the other candidates. Whether you are requesting an interview for a specific position, answering a help-wanted ad, or fishing for job opportunities, keep your cover letter brief and make three main points: identify the job you're writing about, give your strongest qualifications for it, and express your enthusiastic interest in it and how you can be reached. Study the sample résumé cover letters in this chapter.

Address your résumé to the personnel department or the person mentioned in the ad. Send out as many résumés as possible, wherever and whenever you can. Follow their progress on the *Résumé Tracking Sheet* (#62) in the Workbook section.

Many ads are blind boxes. If you don't get a response in ten to fourteen days, send a duplicate résumé. Don't be disheartened by no response at all; firms only follow up for serious interviews.

Résumé Follow-Up

Sending out your résumé is only the first step. You should plan on making a follow-up telephone call within seven days after mailing it. Start with your best prospects first; you can only handle a limited number of calls a day.

When calling, ask for the person who normally receives résumés and when you can speak to him. When you reach that individual, be precise and direct. Make these points:

1. Identify yourself and your reason for calling.
2. Ask if your résumé was received.
3. Suggest a meeting to discuss the position.
4. Try to set up a definite interview during this phone call.
5. If you can arrange an interview, thank him and say goodbye. You've accomplished your aim.
6. If you can't arrange an interview, find out why.
7. If you aren't being considered for the job, be a graceful loser. Send a letter thanking the individual for his time. Always leave the door open for him to call you back.

THE JOB INTERVIEW

The interview is where you win or lose the job. The better prepared you are, the better your odds of getting the job. For a successful interview you should be ready in three areas: likely interview questions, advance knowledge of each prospective employer, and concise, articulate answers. And, needless to say, you should make an attractive, professional appearance.

Interview questions are likely to cover the same general ground, no matter who is asking them. At every interview be prepared to explain why you want the job, why you should be hired, and your long- and short-term career goals. Also be prepared for such provocative questions as, "If you could be anyone in the world, whom would you be?" We've suggested some of these in the *Likely Interview Questions* (#63) worksheet so you can have some answers ready.

Advance knowledge of prospective employers will both prepare you for the particular interview and impress the interviewer with your interest in the company. Use the *Researching Prospective Employers* (#64) worksheet for your findings.

You can get information about a company through various sources:

the company's annual reports, available through the Department of Commerce and its own marketing literature

a Dun & Bradstreet report, available from your local bank, financial advisor, or other Dun & Bradstreet subscriber

the local Chamber of Commerce

Moody's Industrial Manual, at your local library

Encyclopedia of Business Information Sources, at your library

your network contact

your State Information Office of the Department of Employment for a civil service job

Once you have an understanding of the general interview process and the company you're interested in, you'll find it isn't difficult to prepare for an interview. Using your completed worksheets, couple your company research with your general interview answers, and hone the particular points you want to make. Before the all-important job interview, conduct your own question-and-answer session, or ask a friend to role-play a mock meeting with you.

Some Interview Tips

- Plan to arrive at least fifteen minutes early. This gives you time to prepare yourself mentally and avoids in-transit anxiety and possible tardiness. Moreover, there's always the possibility that the interviewer is ahead of schedule and has more time for your meeting. If you're running late, it is imperative that you call.
- Dress appropriately for the position. A fringed suede vest may be fine for a designer, but not for a paralegal.
- Be enthusiastic about the organization and the particular job you want.
- Ask as many questions as possible about the position and the organization. By reversing roles with your interviewer, you're giving him or her a chance to talk, to feel comfortable, and to tell you more about what the company is looking for in an applicant.
- Carry an extra résumé, in case yours was misplaced.
- Leave extra items, like your coat, in the outer office so you can shake hands easily.
- Never make negative remarks about a previous employer. You'll gain nothing except make your prospective employer uneasy about what you'll say about her in the future.

- Suppress any fierce individuality. This is the time to show your team spirit; save your individuality for your supervisor after you get the job.
- Try to avoid stating a salary; let the employer make the first offer. When you name a figure, you risk losing the job if it's too high, or working for less if it's too low. Besides, the person who makes the first offer normally takes less in a negotiation.

The Interview Follow-Up

After the interview, write a pleasant letter thanking the interviewer for her time. See the accompanying sample *Employment Interview Follow-Up Letter* (page 141). This letter (overlooked by most applicants) is not only courteous, it also indicates your continuing interest in the company and puts your name in front of the interviewer one more time.

Get the name of the interviewer's secretary and after four days, make a follow-up call. Find out the best time to talk to the interviewer about your standing for the job.

If you don't get the job, don't let rejection defeat you. Most applicants rarely receive more than one or two job offers in ten interviews.

If you don't get the particular position you want but need a job quickly, take the best that's available. This will relieve some of the financial pressure and give you time for a more complete search.

Samantha Martin
135 Elm Street
San Pedro, California 90503
(213) 555-3171

CAREER DESIRES

To develop a career in management.

CAREER EXPERIENCES

Managed a ten-person office dealing in real estate sales.

Assistant manager of a women's clothing store.

Managed and organized a special fund-raising project for the local school district.

President of the local Parent Teachers Association.

Vice president of Parent Effectiveness Training Group, a local volunteer organization.

EDUCATION

Graduate of San Pedro High School.

Attended University of California at Los Angeles with a major in Business Administration.

REFERENCES

Paul Krueger, owner of Krueger Realty
11200 Inglewood Avenue
Los Angeles, California 90220

Vivian Dondero, personnel manager of ABC Clothing
1258 Westwood Street
West Los Angeles, California 90280

Maryann Rimoin, principal
San Pedro High School
San Pedro, California 90503

Michelle A. Millimet
42 Soundview Drive
Rye, New York 10538
914-555-7858

EXPERIENCE

1981–Present   Shearson Lehman Brothers, Corporate Finance
Department

Assistant Associate

Responsible for new business brochure. Compiled
statistics for potential stock and bond offerings.
Helped prepare prospectuses for new offerings.

1979–1981   State University of New York, Purchase, New York

Editorial Assistant

Assisted Chairman of Economics Department with
course materials and statistical monographs.

1972–1977   Westchester General Hospital, Port Chester, New
York

Administrator

Prepared and administered budgets and grants.

Assistant, Accounting Department

Kept records of hospital supplies and purchases, other
billing responsibilities.

EDUCATION

State University of New York, Purchase, New York
B. A. Economics, 1977–1981

Lasell Junior College, Auburndale, Massachusetts
Associate in Arts, 1959–1961

COMMUNITY ACTIVITIES

Docent, Newberger Museum, Purchase, New York

Board member/chairwoman, Auxiliary of Westchester
Children's Health Center

Michelle A. Millimet—Resume
Page 2

                        Volunteer teacher's aide, Rye, New York, School
                        District

References   Available upon request

Jennifer Martin
1208 North Boulevard
St. Louis, Missouri 63117
·(314) 555-3171

PUBLIC RELATIONS

Helped plan a major women's business conference for over 400
participants and moderated a panel on re-entering the job market.

Researched and contacted speakers, organized monthly programs, wrote
news releases, and introduced the speakers for a large professional
organization.

COMMUNITY RELATIONS

Promoted a fund-raising organization by contacting and soliciting the
participation of key people in the community. Established a scholarship
committee and worked with the financial aid staff to grant scholarships.
Over five years, donations rose from $100,000 to $350,000.

RESEARCH

Designed and conducted a survey to assess the needs of the members of a
professional group. Results of the survey enabled the group to determine
how best to meet its goals and objectives.

Researched and wrote a paper concerning Physiological and
Environmental Factors that Influence Scholastic Performance. Conducted
background research, collected and analyzed data. Presented the paper to
the Missouri Psychological Association.

MANAGEMENT AND ADMINISTRATION

Promoted to director of dormitory because of ability to negotiate for an
equitable duty schedule and promote a team spirit among staff.

Acted as liaison between a variety of diverse groups, and was responsible
for 400 undergraduate students.

Jennifer Martin—Resume
Page 2

WORK HISTORY

8/81–Present	Coordinator, Hotline, Drug Abuse Center, City of St. Louis, Missouri
6/59–8/64	Research Associate, Department of Environmental Studies, Webster College, Webster Groves, Missouri
8/57–6/59	Research Assistant, Department of Psychology, St. Louis University
9/56–8/57	Resident Advisor, Department of Psychology, St. Louis University

PROFESSIONAL AFFILIATIONS

United Way Campaign Committee, Chairwoman, St. Louis
League of Women Voters
American Association of University Women
    Program Development Chairwoman

VOLUNTEER ACTIVITIES

Junior League, St. Louis
Child Abuse Crisis Center, Children's Bureau of St. Louis
Hotline, Drug Abuse Center, St. Louis

EDUCATION
B.A. in Psychology, St. Louis University, St. Louis, Missouri

Personnel Director
ABC Corporation
Los Angeles, California

Dear Sir:

I would like to be considered for the position of _____

as advertised in _____ on _____ .

Enclosed is a résumé outlining my background and qualifications.

You will note that my experience as a _____
makes me well qualified for this position.

If my qualifications are of interest to you, I can arrange for a personal
interview at your convenience. I will contact you within the next five days
to discuss this opportunity.

Very truly yours,

Dear _____:

_____ suggested I contact you for the position of

_____.

I have enclosed a résumé outlining my background and qualifications for this position.

I will contact you in the next few days to arrange for a meeting to discuss this opportunity.

Very truly yours,

始始

Reassurance Associates
1 Insurance Square
Center City, Iowa

Reassurance Associates
1 Insurance Square
Center City, Iowa

Dear _____ :

Thank you for the time you spent with me outlining the job functions and explaining the details of your company's operations.

I am enthusiastic about this position and your company. It offers the opportunity for the long-term employment and personal growth that I desire.

Please let me know if you need any additional information. I will be in touch with your office to answer any questions that you might have.

Very truly yours,

SUGGESTED READING & SOURCES OF INFORMATION

Chapter 1. Keeping Family Records and Documents

Action for Independent Maturity (AIM), Division of the American Association of Retired Persons (AARP), 1909 K Street, N.W., Washington, D.C. 20049.

———. "Guide to Your Vital Papers and Where to Find Them." Both are free.

———. "Your Vital Papers Logbook."

Consumer Information Center, P.O. Box 100, Pueblo, CO 81002.

———. "Keeping Family-Household Records: What to Discard." #638F.

Superintendent of Documents, U.S. Government Printing Office, Dept. 33, Washington, D.C. 20402. General Services Administration.

———. "Guide to Record Retention." $3.00. Outlines how long businesses and private citizens should retain various types of records.

———. "Where to Write for Vital Records: Births, Deaths, Marriages, Divorces" (1982). U.S. Department of Health and Human Services. S/N 017-022-00794-1. 18 pp. $3.25. State-by-state listings of application offices and fees for obtaining certified copies of birth, death, marriage, and divorce records.

Chapter 2. Picking Your Advisory Team

American Bar Association, 1155 East 60th Street, Chicago, IL 60637.

American Institute of Certified Public Accountants (AICPA), 1211 Avenue of the Americas, New York, NY 10036. Professional society of accountants certified by the states and territories.

Burnett, Barbara A. *Every Woman's Legal Guide*. New York: Doubleday, 1983. 600 pp. $19.95. How women can use the legal system, including a glossary of terms and list of national hotlines.

Hermann, Philip J. *Do You Need a Lawyer?* Englewood Cliffs, N.J.: Prentice-Hall, 1980. 160 pp. $4.95. How to determine if you require legal counsel and how to choose an attorney to suit your needs.

Institute of Certified Financial Planners, 3443 South Galena, Suite 190, Denver, CO 80231. Individuals who qualify as CFPs.

International Association of Financial Planners, 5775 Peachtree Dunwoody Road, Suite 120-C, Atlanta, GA 30342.

Investors Service Bureau, New York Stock Exchange, 11 Wall Street, New York, NY 10005.
———. "How to Get Help When You Invest," and an Investor's Kit for $3.50.

Martindale-Hubbell Law Directory. Complete annual legal directory services. Lists of firms and lawyers of the U.S. and foreign countries, including biographical information.

National Association of Enrolled Federal Tax Accountants, 6108 North Harding Avenue, Chicago, IL 60659.

National Association of Securities Dealers (NASD), 1735 K Street, N.W., Washington, D.C. 20006. Investment brokers and dealers authorized to conduct transactions of the investment banking and securities business under federal and state laws. Publishes monthly, quarterly, and annual reports.

National Society of Public Accountants, 1010 North Fairfax Street, Alexandria, VA 22314. Professional society of public accountants. Publishes brochure and portfolio of accounting systems for small- and medium-size businesses.

Office of Consumer Securities and Exchange Commission, Securities and Exchange Commission, 500 North Capitol Street, N.W., Washington, D.C. 20549. This department processes complaints and inquiries from investors and the public.

Securities and Exchange Commission, 500 North Capitol Street, N.W., Washington, D.C. 20549. Contact this agency with problems involving securities transactions.

Standard & Poor's, 25 Broadway, New York, NY 10004. Reference materials on stocks and bonds, and bond ratings.

Chapter 3. Figuring Your Net Worth

American Association of Retired Persons (AARP/NRTA), 1909 K Street, N.W., Washington, D.C. 20049.
———. "Tax Facts."
———. "Your Retirement Income Tax Guide." Both are free.

Consumer Information Center, P.O. Box 100, Pueblo, CO 81002.
———. "A Guide to Individual Retirement Accounts" (1981). #183N. 9 pp. $2.00.

Kelly Blue Book: Auto Market Report. A bimonthly periodical, the official guide to used cars.

Pension Benefit Guaranty Corporation, 2020 K Street, N.W., Washington, D.C. 20006.
———. "Information on Individual Retirement Accounts and Keogh Plans." Free.
———. "What Every Investor Should Know" (1982). #185N. 43pp. $4.50. Describes different types of securities, including stocks, bonds, mutual funds, and treasury notes.

Chapter 4. Banking

Community and Fair Lending Examinations Division, Comptroller of the Currency, Department of the Treasury, Washington, D.C. 20219. Contact this office with problems involving the practices of any national bank.

Cook, John A., and Robert Wool. *All You Need to Know About Banks*. New York: Bantam, 1983. 202 pp. $13.95.

Division of Consumer Affairs, Washington, D.C. 20551. Contact this agency with problems regarding a state-chartered bank's practices.

Division of Consumer Affairs, National Credit Union Administration, Washington, D.C. 20546. Contact this agency with problems concerning credit.

Elliott, Peter. *Questions and Answers in Banking*. Dover, N.H.: Woodhead-Faulkner, 1984. 128 pp. $11.95.

Office of Community Investment, Federal Home Loan Bank Board, Washington, D.C. 20552. Contact this agency with problems concerning savings and loan associations.

Weinstein, Grace W. *The Lifetime Book of Money Management*. New York: New American Library, 1983. 672 pp. $19.50.

Chapter 5. Borrowing

Alexander, Don H. *How to Borrow Money From a Bank: Banking for the Non-Banker*. New York: Beauford Books, 1984. 96 pp. $7.95.

American Express, Box 927, New York, NY 10010.
————. "The Credit Handbook for Women." Free.

Chapter 6. Establishing Credit

Bank of America, Box 37128, San Francisco, CA 94137.
————. "How to Establish Credit," Consumer Information Report 3.
————. "Shopping for Adjustable-Rate Credit," Consumer Information Report 31.

Block, Elizabeth J. *A Woman's Guide to Credit*. New York: Ace Books, 1982. 224 pp. $3.25.

Commercial Credit, 300 St. Paul Place, Baltimore, MD 21202.
————. "Women to Your Credit." Free.

Consumer Information Center, P.O. Box 100, Pueblo, CO 81002.
————. "Alice in Debitland: Consumer Protections and Electronic Banking" (1980). #589N. 16 pp. Free. Discusses bank cards and how to protect yourself against computer error and theft.
————. "The Arithmetic of Interest Rates" (1984). #418N. 33 pp. Guide to understanding and calculating compound interest rates.
————. "Consumer Credit Handbook" (1982). #591N. 44 pp. Free. How to apply for credit, what to do if you are denied, and the laws that protect you.
————. "Fair Credit Billing" (1978). #419N. 3 pp. $.50. How to handle billing disputes on credit card purchases.
————. "Fair Credit Reporting Act" (1980). #420N. 3 pp. $.50. How to verify the data in your credit file, and what to do if you are denied based on inaccurate information.

Federal Trade Commission, Pennsylvania Avenue at Sixth Street, N.W., Washington, D.C. 20580. Contact this agency with problems with credit cards, retail stores, or finance companies.

Superintendent of Documents, U.S. Government Printing Office, Dept. 33, Washington, D.C. 20402.

————. "A Citizen's Guide on How to Use the Freedom of Information Act and the Privacy Act in Requesting Government Documents" (1977). U.S. House of Representatives/House Committee on Government Operations. S/N 052-071-00540-4. 59 pp. $4.50. Tells how to request records, which act to use, and provides sample request and appeal letters.

————. "Do You Speak Credit?" (1982). Federal Trade Commission, Bureau of Consumer Protection. S/N 018-000-00290-6. 13 pp. $2.75. A plain English explanation of the twelve common legal clauses used in credit contracts.

Chapter 7. Budgeting

Brien, Mimi. *Moneywise*. New York: Bantam Books, 1982. $3.50.

Briles, Judith. *The Woman's Guide to Financial Savvy*, rev. ed. New York: St. Martin's Press, 1982. 240 pp. $6.95.

————. *Money Phases: The Six Financial Stages of a Woman's Life*. New York: Simon & Schuster, 1984. 224 pp. $14.95.

Miller, Theodore J., ed. *Make Your Money Grow: Smart Steps to Success in the Exciting Years Ahead*, rev. ed. New York: Dell, 1984. 528 pp. $8.95.

Minkow, Rosalie. *Money Management for Women*. New York: Jove Pub., 1981. 256 pp. $2.50.

Porter, Sylvia. *Sylvia Porter's Your Own Money*. New York: Avon Books, 1983. 768 pp. $12.95.

Roehm, A. *Spending Less and Enjoying It More: How to Get Control of Your Money*. New York: McGraw-Hill, 1984. 177 pp. $8.95.

Siverd, Bonnie. *Count Your Change: A Woman's Guide to Sudden Financial Change*. Chicago: Priam Books, 1983. 180 pp. $6.95.

Weinstein, Grace W. *The Lifetime Book of Money Management*. New York: New American Library, 1983. 672 pp. $19.50.

Chapter 8. Planning Your Estate

Becker, Benjamin M., and Ben M. Roth. *A Simplified Approach to Planning Estates: Problems and Solutions*. Rockville Center, N.Y.: Farnsworth Pub., 1982. 204 pp. $12.95.

Clay, William C., Jr. *The Dow Jones-Irwin Guide to Estate Planning*, 6th ed. Homewood, Illinois: Dow Jones-Irwin, 1984. 166 pp. $14.95.

Harris, Ollie K., and Elizabeth Slover. *So Let It Be*. Nacogdoches, Texas: Ericson Books, 1982. $12.50.

Howell, Cotton. *How to Write Your Own Will*. Los Angeles: Liberty Pub., 1984. 176 pp. $9.95.

Hughes, Theodore E., and David Klein. *A Family Guide to Estate Planning, Funeral Arrangements & Settling an Estate After Death*. New York: Scribner, 1983. 240 pp. $15.95.

Kahn, Arnold D. *Family Security Through Estate Planning*, 2nd ed. New York: McGraw-Hill, 1983. 224 pp. $19.95. Answers concerning life insurance, wills, trusts, and estate and gift taxes.

Lasser, J. K. *J. K. Lasser's Your Estate & Gift Taxes*. New York: Simon & Schuster, 1985. 265 pp. $15.95.

Magee, David S. *Everything Your Heirs Need to Know About You*. Naperville, Illinois: Caroline House, 1982. $9.95.

Pladsen, Carol, and Denis Clifford. *The Family Records Book*. Berkeley: Nolo Press, 1984. 208 pp. $12.95.

Plotnick, Charles, and Stephan Leimberg. *Get Rich—Stay Rich: Making It, Passing It Along Under the New Tax Laws*. Briarcliff Manor, N.Y.: Stein & Day, 1984. 352 pp. $9.95.

Starr, Herbert F. *Estate Planning Made Easy*. Los Angeles: Liberty Pub., 1984. 160 pp. $9.95.

Chapter 9.   Distributing Your Assets

Consumer Information Center, P.O. Box 100, Pueblo, CO 81002.
———. "Providing for Your Heirs—Non-Sale Property Transfers." #429N. 7 pp. $.50. Discusses estate and inheritance taxes, the cost of administering an estate, and legal tools such as wills, trusts, joint ownerships, and gifts.

Dukeminier, Jesse, and Stanley Johanson. *Wills, Trusts & Estates*, 3rd ed. Boston: Little, Brown & Company, 1984. 1140 pp. $32.00.

Internal Revenue Service, 1111 Constitution Ave., N.W., Washington, D.C. 20224.
———. "Federal Tax Guide for Survivors, Executors and Administrators." Publication #559. Free.

Jentz, Barry C. *Entry: The Hiring, Start-Up & Supervision of Administrators*. New York: McGraw-Hill, 1982. 256 pp. $15.95.

Mathew Bender Publishers. *Automated Will Drafting:* Release 1 (#603); Release 3 (#602) 1983. Write for information: Mathew Bender Publishers, 235 East 45th Street, New York, NY 10014.

Rehrer, Mervin. *My Will Be Done*. New York: Vantage, 1984. $9.95.

Soled, Alex J. *The Essential Guide to Wills, Estates, Trusts and Death Taxes*. Glenview, Illinois: Scott, Foresman & Company, 1981. 248 pp. $12.95.

Starchild, Adam. *Building Wealth: A Layman's Guide to Trust Planning*. Chicago: American Management Assn., 1981. 192 pp. $15.95.

Chapter 10.   Childproof: Protecting Your Child

Apolloni, Tony, and Thomas P. Cooke., eds. *A New Look at Guardianship: Protective Services that Support Personalized Living*. Des Moines, Iowa: PH Books, 1984. 360 pp. $24.95.

Faber, Stuart J. *Handbook of Guardianships & Conservatorships*, 4th ed. Los Angeles: Legal Books, 1984. $28.50.

Internal Revenue Service, 1111 Constitution Ave., N.W., Washington, D.C. 20224.
———. "A Guide to Federal Estate and Gift Taxation." (#448). Free.

MacKay, Richard V., and Irving J. Sloan., eds. *The Law of Guardianships*, 3rd ed. Dobbs Ferry, N.Y.: Oceana, 1980. 125 pp. $5.95.

Weinstein, Grace W. *Children & Money: A Parent's Guide*. New York: New American Library/Plume, 1985. $8.95.

Chapter 11.   The Role of Life Insurance

Best's Insurance Reports, A.M. Best Company, Inc. Oldwick, N.J. 08858. *Best's Review*. Ratings of insurance companies on their management and financial stability.

Brownlie, William D. *Life Insurance: Its Rate of Return*. Cincinnati: National Underwriter, 1983. 201 pp. $13.45.

Consumer Information Center, P.O. Box 100, Pueblo, CO 81002.

Consumer Reports Editors. *The Consumers Union Report of Life Insurance: A Guide to Planning & Buying the Protection You Need*. New York: Holt, Rinehart & Winston, 1981. 384 pp. $8.95.

Consumer's Reports, 256 Washington St., Mt. Vernon, N.Y. 10553.
———. "A Consumer's Guide to Life Insurance" (1983). #592N. 21 pp. Free.

Kenton, Walter S., Jr. *How Life Insurance Companies Rob You and What You Can Do About It*. New York: Random House, 1983. $13.95.

Kessler, Ronald. *The Life Insurance Game*. New York: Holt, Rinehart & Winston, 1985. 320 pp. $15.95.

Tobias, Andrew. *The Invisible Bankers: Everything You Always Wanted to Know About Insurance, But Were Afraid to Ask*. New York: Pocket Books, 1983. $3.95.

Chapter 12.   Serious Illness

Eusebio, Thomas C. *Guide to Health Insurance*. Indianapolis: Rough Notes, 1981. $12.00.

Gaines, Price, ed. *Time Saver for Disability Income & Health Insurance*. Cincinnati: National Underwriter, 1984. 278 pp. $17.10.

Weinstein, Grace W. *The Lifetime Book of Money Management*, New York: New American Library, 1983. $19.50.

Chapter 13.   Disability

Gaines, Price, ed. *Time Saver for Disability Income & Health Insurance*. Cincinnati: National Underwriter, 1984. 278 pp. $17.10.

Soule, Charles E. *Disability Income Insurance: The Unique Risks*. Homewood, Illinois: Dow Jones-Irwin, 1984. 238 pp. $22.50.

Superintendent of Documents, U.S. Government Printing Office, Dept. 33, Washington, D.C. 20402.
———. "Pocket Guide to Federal Help for the Disabled Person." U.S. Department of Education (1983). S/N 065-000-00193-4. 23 pp. $1.75.

Chapter 14.   Property Loss and Other Accidents

Consumer Information Center, P.O. Box 100, Pueblo, CO 81002.
———. "In Time of Emergency" (1983). #430N. 38 pp. $0.50. Advice on protecting life, property, and health from natural and man-made disasters.

Fessler, George R., and Ray D. Westcott. *The Insurance Primer: Fire and Casualty,* 13th ed. Phoenix: Primer Publications, 1984. 172 pp. $7.95.

Gee, Harold F. *An Approach to Property & Casualty Insurance.* Indianapolis: Rough Notes, 1980. $8.00.

Huebner, S. S., et al. *Property and Liability Insurance,* 3rd ed. Indianapolis: Rough Notes, 1982. $12.00.

Superintendent of Documents, U.S. Government Printing Office, Dept. 33, Washington, D.C. 20402.
———. "After the Fire: Returning to Normal." Federal Emergency Management Agency (1980). S/N 064-000-00019-5. 13 pp. $2.75. Discusses insurance coverage, recordkeeping, and reimbursable expenses.

Weinstein, Grace W. *The Lifetime Book of Money Management.* New York: New American Library, 1983. $19.50.

Chapter 15. Auto Protection

Kohl, James A. *How to Save Money on Your Auto Insurance.* Helena, Montana: Jaks Publishing Co., 1980. 88 pp. $10.00.

Majka, Paul. *You Can Save a Bundle on Your Car Insurance.* New York: St. Martin's Press, 1982. 96 pp. $3.95.

Chapter 16. When a Death Occurs

Consumer Information Center, P.O. Box 100, Pueblo, CO 81002.
———. "A Woman's Guide to Social Security" (1983). #514N. 16 pp. Free. Benefits on retirement, widowhood, divorce.
———. "Your Social Security" (1984). #515N. 36 pp. Free. Who is eligible and how to get benefits.

Fisher, Ida, and Byron Lane. *Widow's Guide to Life: How to Adjust/How to Grow.* Long Beach, Ca.: Lane Con Press, 1985. 207 pp. $8.95.

Social Security Administration, 6401 Security Boulevard, Baltimore, MD 21235, or local Social Security Administration Office. For information about replacement of earnings lost to dependents because of retirement; because of worker's death or physical/mental impairment severe enough to prevent a person from working.

Chapter 17. Using Your Survival Instincts

Morgan, Marie. *Breaking Through: How to Overcome Housewives' Depression.* Winston Press, 1983. 204 pp. $8.95.

Scobey, Joan. *I'm a Stranger Here Myself: The Panic (and Pleasure) of Middle Age.* New York: St. Martin's Press/Marek, 1984. $12.95.

Selye, Hans, M. D. *Stress Without Distress.* New York: Signet, 1975. $2.95.

Yates, Martha. *Coping: A Survival Manual for Women Alone.* Englewood Cliffs, N.J.: Prentice-Hall, 1976. $4.95.

Zimney, Connie F. *In Praise of Homemaking: Affirming the Choice to Be a Mother-at-Home.* Notre Dame, Indiana: Ave Maria, 1984. $4.95.

Chapter 18.   The Job Market

Bolles, Richard Nelson. *What Color Is Your Parachute? A Practical Guide for Job Hunters & Career Changers,* 2nd ed. Berkeley, Calif.: Ten Speed Press, 1984. 384 pp. $8.95.

Business and Professional Women's Foundation, 2012 Massachusetts Avenue, N.W., Washington, D.C. 20036. "Dedicated to improving the economic status of working women through their integration into all occupations." Awards educational scholarships to mature women. Established by National Federation of Business and Professional Women's Clubs. Issues publications list.

Catalyst, 14 East 60th Street, New York, NY 10022. "To develop and expand career options for women and to increase corporate awareness of women as a resource." Among the forty self-guidance opportunity booklets it publishes are:

The Catalyst Staff. *Marketing Yourself: The Catalyst Women's Guide to Successful Résumés and Interviews.* New York: Bantam, 1981. 224 pp. $3.95.

———. *Making the Most of Your First Job.* New York: Ballantine, 1982. 240 pp. $2.75.

———. *What to Do With the Rest of Your Life: The Catalyst Career Guide for Women in the 80's.* New York: Simon & Schuster, 1981. $9.95.

———. *When Can You Start? The Complete Job Search Guide for Women of All Ages.* New York: Macmillan, 1982. 148 pp. $9.95.

Douglass, Donna N. *Choice & Compromise: A Woman's Guide to Balancing Family & Career.* Chicago: American Management Assn., 1983. 208 pp. $8.95.

Fader, Shirley Sloan. *From Kitchen to Career.* Briarcliff Manor, N.Y.: Stein & Day, 1977.

Holz, Herman. *Beyond the Résumé: How to Land the Job You Want.* New York: McGraw-Hill Paperbacks, 1984. 256 pp. $7.95.

National Federation of Business and Professional Women's Clubs, 2012 Massachusetts Avenue, N.W., Washington, D.C. 20036. Business and professional women representing 300 occupations. Publishes bimonthly *National Business Women.*

National Organization of Women (NOW), 425 13th Street, N.W., Suite 723, Washington, D.C. 20004. Publishes monthly *National Now Times.*

NOW Legal Defense and Education Fund, 132 West 43rd Street, New York, NY 10036. The educational and litigating affiliate of NOW. Publishes brochures and pamphlets.

Wider Opportunities for Women (WOW), 1325 G Street, N.W., Lower Level, Washington, D.C. 20005. "To expand employment opportunities for women through information, employment training, and advocacy services." Publishes *Connections* newsletter, *Working for You: A Guide to Employing Women in Non-Traditional Jobs,* as well as other books and pamphlets.

The Working Woman Report: Succeeding in Business in the Eighties. Editors of *Working Woman* and Gay Bryant. New York: Simon & Schuster, 1984. $15.95.

ABOUT THE AUTHORS

Don Martin is the president and cofounder of Cal-Surance Associates, Inc., the largest privately held insurance brokerage firm in California. Founded twenty-three years ago, Cal-Surance is thirtieth in size in the nation. Don Martin is a sought-after speaker at insurance and finance seminars across the country.

During Renee Martin's successful ten-year career as a real-estate broker, she became aware of the lack of information available to women facing family crises. This realization led her to redirect her energies toward helping women through her writing, community work, counseling, and lecturing.

Combining their talents, Don and Renee devoted three years of research and great personal committment to A SURVIVAL KIT FOR WIVES. Their hope is that it will help women to be secure, knowledgeable, and self-sufficient.

WORKBOOK

WORKSHEETS AND CHECKLISTS

This workbook is perforated so you have the choice of working in the book or detaching the pages. If you need additional copies of any page—for updating your information, for correcting errors, for your own note taking, or just to have a complete set on hand (and that's a good idea)—you can duplicate the pages right from the book, or remove them first, if you prefer.

#18 Interview Questions for Financial Institutions
#19 Financial Institution Evaluation Guide
#20 Collateral Guarantee or Co-Signature Record
#21 Loan Interest Rate Comparison
#22 Emergency Cash Plan
#23 Daily Cash Budgeting Worksheet
#24 Monthly Expense Budgeting Worksheet
#25 Annual Expense Budgeting Worksheet
#26 Discretionary Expense Worksheet
#27 Monthly Budget Control Worksheet
#28 List of Ownership of Assets
#29 Estate Planning Checklist
#30 Will Preparation Worksheet
#31 When to Review a Will
#32 Evaluation Guide: Individual Executor or Trustee
#33 Evaluation Guide: Institutional Executor or Trustee
#34 Evaluation Guide: Guardian of the Person
#35 Evaluation Guide: Guardian of the Estate
#36 Trustee Evaluation Guide
#37 Childproof Protection Summary
#38 Life Insurance Worksheet
#39 Dependent Income Worksheet
#40 Beneficiary Worksheet
#41 Medical Insurance Coverage Worksheet
#42 Medical Insurance Cost/Coverage Comparison
#43 Evaluating HMO and Group Insurance
#44 Disability Insurance Checklist
#45 Emergency Disability Plan
#46 Long-Term Disability Plan
#47 Household Inventory Record
#48 Special Inventory: Record of Jewelry, Silverware, Art
#49 Homeowner's Insurance Checklist
#50 Homeowner's Insurance Cost Comparison Worksheet
#51 Property Loss Reporting Form
#52 Accident Reporting Form
#53 Automobile Insurance Checklist
#54 Insurance Premium Cost Comparison
#55 Automobile Accident Reporting Form
#56 Transition Plan Checklist
    At Once
    Within the First 30 Days
    Within the Next 60 Days
    Within the Next 6 Months

LOCATION OF IMPORTANT PAPERS

Completed as of _____

Type of Document	Location				Length of Time to Keep
	Home File	Safe-Deposit Box	Office	Other	
1. PERSONAL					
Certificate of birth	[ ]	[ ]	[ ]	[ ]	Permanently
Certificate of marriage	[ ]	[ ]	[ ]	[ ]	Permanently
Certificate of divorce	[ ]	[ ]	[ ]	[ ]	Permanently
Social Security cards	[ ]	[ ]	[ ]	[ ]	Permanently
Military discharge	[ ]	[ ]	[ ]	[ ]	Permanently
Passports	[ ]	[ ]	[ ]	[ ]	Permanently
Wills	[ ]	[ ]	[ ]	[ ]	Permanently
Death certificate	[ ]	[ ]	[ ]	[ ]	Permanently
2. FINANCIAL					
Bank account information	[ ]	[ ]	[ ]	[ ]	7 years
Loan agreements	[ ]	[ ]	[ ]	[ ]	While in force

LOCATION OF IMPORTANT PAPERS (Cont.)

Completed as of _____

Type of Document	Home File	Safe-Deposit Box	Office	Other	Length of Time to Keep
Stocks and bonds	[ ]	[ ]	[ ]	[ ]	Permanently
Government securities	[ ]	[ ]	[ ]	[ ]	Permanently
Notes due to others or you	[ ]	[ ]	[ ]	[ ]	Length of note
Passbooks	[ ]	[ ]	[ ]	[ ]	While in force
Pension or profit-sharing plan information	[ ]	[ ]	[ ]	[ ]	Permanently
IRA and Keogh plan	[ ]	[ ]	[ ]	[ ]	Permanently
Other items _____	[ ]	[ ]	[ ]	[ ]	_____
_____	[ ]	[ ]	[ ]	[ ]	_____
_____	[ ]	[ ]	[ ]	[ ]	_____

3. TAXES

Type of Document	Home File	Safe-Deposit Box	Office	Other	Length of Time to Keep
Past returns	[ ]	[ ]	[ ]	[ ]	7 years
Canceled checks	[ ]	[ ]	[ ]	[ ]	7 years

Location columns: Home File, Safe-Deposit Box, Office, Other

Other _____
_____

4. INSURANCE

Life insurance policies	[ ]	[ ]	[ ]	Permanently
Homeowners policy	[ ]	[ ]	[ ]	1 year
Auto policy	[ ]	[ ]	[ ]	1 year
Major Medical	[ ]	[ ]	[ ]	1 year
Other _____	[ ]	[ ]	[ ]	

5. REAL ESTATE

Trust deeds	[ ]	[ ]	[ ]	Permanently
Real estate notes	[ ]	[ ]	[ ]	Permanently
Title policy	[ ]	[ ]	[ ]	Permanently
Mortgage documents	[ ]	[ ]	[ ]	Permanently
Tax assessments	[ ]	[ ]	[ ]	7 years
Rental agreements	[ ]	[ ]	[ ]	3 years
Rental receipts	[ ]	[ ]	[ ]	3 years
Receipts for repairs	[ ]	[ ]	[ ]	3 years
Receipts for improvements	[ ]	[ ]	[ ]	Permanently

LOCATION OF IMPORTANT PAPERS (Cont.)

Completed as of _____

Type of Document	Location				Length of Time to Keep
	Home File	Safe-Deposit Box	Office	Other	
Other _____	[ ]	[ ]	[ ]	[ ]	_____
_____	[ ]	[ ]	[ ]	[ ]	_____
6. MEDICAL					
Records	[ ]	[ ]	[ ]	[ ]	Permanently
Receipts	[ ]	[ ]	[ ]	[ ]	1 year
Insurance payments	[ ]	[ ]	[ ]	[ ]	1 year
7. AUTOS					
Registration	[ ]	[ ]	[ ]	[ ]	Until sold
Ownership	[ ]	[ ]	[ ]	[ ]	Until sold
Loan agreement	[ ]	[ ]	[ ]	[ ]	3 years
Loan payment records	[ ]	[ ]	[ ]	[ ]	1 year
Lease agreement	[ ]	[ ]	[ ]	[ ]	Length of lease
Repair records	[ ]	[ ]	[ ]	[ ]	3 years

8. SAFE-DEPOSIT BOX
INFO

[ ]   [ ]   [ ]   [ ]   _____ Permanently

_____
_____
_____

Persons authorized:

_____
_____
_____

9. POWER OF ATTORNEY
Names

[ ]   [ ]   _____ Permanently

_____
_____
_____

10. MISCELLANEOUS ITEMS

Survival Kit for Wives

[ ]   [ ]   [ ]   [ ]   _____ Permanently

[ ]   [ ]   [ ]   [ ]   _____

[ ]   [ ]   [ ]   [ ]   _____

[ ]   [ ]   [ ]   [ ]   _____

_____
_____
_____

LOCATION OF IMPORTANT PAPERS (Cont.)

Completed as of _____

Type of Document	Location				Length of Time to Keep
	Home File	Safe-Deposit Box	Office	Other	
_____	▢	▢	▢	▢	_____
_____	▢	▢	▢	▢	_____
_____	▢	▢	▢	▢	_____
_____	▢	▢	▢	▢	_____
_____	▢	▢	▢	▢	_____

Special remarks: _____
_____
_____
_____
_____

For more information, see page 5.

BANKING INFORMATION
Completed as of _____

Name of Bank	Account No.	Branch	Address	Bank Contact	Type of Account: Joint (J), Husband (H), Wife (W), Trust (T)	Checking (C), Savings (S), Money Market (M)

For more information, see page 7.

LIST OF STOCK SECURITIES
As of

Name of Security	No. of Shares	Owner	Type	Original Cost	Current Value per Share	Total Current Value
				$	$	$

For more information, see page 7.

LIST OF BOND SECURITIES
As of _____

Type	Owner	Interest Rate	Due Date	$

For more information, see page 7.

CURRENT INSURANCE POLICIES

For the year

_____

Insurance for:	Insuring Company	Policy No.	Expiration Date
Automobiles (Liability, Fire, Theft, Collision)	_____	_____	_____
Residence Building	_____	_____	_____
Contents	_____	_____	_____
Second Home	_____	_____	_____
Liability to Others (Non-auto)	_____	_____	_____
Extra Liability Limits (Personal Umbrella)	_____	_____	_____
Medical and Surgical	_____	_____	_____
Major Medical	_____	_____	_____
Excess Major Medical	_____	_____	_____
Life Insurance	_____	_____	_____
	_____	_____	_____
	_____	_____	_____
	_____	_____	_____
	_____	_____	_____
Disability	_____	_____	_____
Other	_____	_____	_____

For more information, see page 7.

REAL ESTATE PROPERTIES

As of _____

Property Address	Description 1. Home 2. Vacation Home 3. Commercial 4. Industrial 5. Residential Investment	Approxi- mate Value	Holder of Loan
1.			
2.			
3.			
4.			
5.			

REAL ESTATE PROPERTIES (Cont.)

As of _____

Property Address	Description 1. Home 2. Vacation Home 3. Commercial 4. Industrial 5. Residential Investment	Approxi-mate Value	Holder of Loan
6.			
7.			
8.			

For more information, see page 8.

SAFE-DEPOSIT BOX INFORMATION AND CONTENTS

Compiled as of

_____

Location of Box: _____

_____

Key No.: _____

Locations of Keys: _____

_____

_____

Persons Authorized to Enter the Box:

_____

_____

_____

_____

Contents of Box: _____

_____

_____

_____

_____

_____

_____

_____

_____

_____

_____

For more information, see page 8.

FAMILY
STATUS
RECORD

As of

_____

Husband's Name: _____

Date of Birth: _____ _Soc. Sec. #_ _____

Wife's Name: _____

Date of Birth: _____ _Soc. Sec. #_ _____

Home Address: _____

Business Address: _(H)_ _____

_(W)_ _____

Children's Names and Addresses	Sex	Date of Birth	Married, Divorced, or Single	Soc. Sec. #
_____	__	_____	_____	_____
_____				
_____	__	_____	_____	_____
_____				
_____	__	_____	_____	_____
_____				
_____	__	_____	_____	_____
_____				
_____	__	_____	_____	_____
_____				

FAMILY STATUS RECORD (Cont.)

As of

_____

Grandchildren's Names and Addresses	Sex	Date of Birth	Married, Divorced, or Single	Soc. Sec. #
_____	__	_____	_____	_____
_____	__	_____	_____	_____
_____	__	_____	_____	_____
_____	__	_____	_____	_____
_____	__	_____	_____	_____
_____	__	_____	_____	_____
_____	__	_____	_____	_____
_____	__	_____	_____	_____

Others to Be Considered: Names and Addresses	Sex	Date of Birth	Relationship	Soc. Sec. #
_____	__	_____	_____	_____
_____	__	_____	_____	_____
_____	__	_____	_____	_____
_____	__	_____	_____	_____
_____	__	_____	_____	_____
_____	__	_____	_____	_____
_____	__	_____	_____	_____

For more information,
see page 9.

NOTES
INFORMATION

NOTES DUE YOU

Person Owing	Amount	Due Date	Interest Rate
_____	_____	_____	_____
_____	_____	_____	_____
_____	_____	_____	_____

Additional information on notes: _____

_____

_____

NOTES DUE OTHERS

Owed to	Amount	Due Date	Interest Rate
_____	_____	_____	_____
_____	_____	_____	_____
_____	_____	_____	_____

Additional information on notes: _____

_____

_____

For more information, see page 9.

LIST OF
CREDIT CARDS
Compiled as of _____

Name of Card	Card #	Expiration Date	Authorized Card Users	Telephone Contact if Lost or Stolen

For more information, see page 10.

LIST OF IMPORTANT ADVISORS

As of

_____

Personal Attorney: _____

Name of Firm: _____

Address: _____

Telephone (Bus.) _____ (Res.) _____

Business Attorney: _____

Name of Firm: _____

Address: _____

Telephone (Bus.) _____ (Res.) _____

Personal Accountant: _____

Name of Firm: _____

Address: _____

Telephone (Bus.) _____ (Res.) _____

Personal Banker: _____

Name of Bank: _____

Address: _____

Telephone (Bus.) _____ (Res.) _____

Life Insurance Agent: _____

Name of Firm: _____

Address: _____

Telephone (Bus.) _____ (Res.) _____

LIST OF IMPORTANT ADVISORS (Cont.)

As of

_____

Automobile Agent: _____

Name of Firm: _____

Address: _____

Telephone (Bus.) _____ (Res.) _____

Homeowner's Insurance Agent: _____

Name of Firm: _____

Address: _____

Telephone (Bus.) _____ (Res.) _____

Investment Advisor: _____

Name of Firm: _____

Address: _____

Telephone (Bus.) _____ (Res.) _____

Doctor's Name: _____

Address: _____

Telephone (Bus.) _____ (Res.) _____

Specialty: _____

Doctor's Name: _____

Address: _____

Telephone (Bus.) _____ (Res.) _____

Specialty: _____

Doctor's Name: _____

Address: _____

Telephone (Bus.) _____ (Res.) _____

Specialty: _____

Dentist's Name: _____

Address: _____

Telephone (Bus.) _____ (Res.) _____

LIST OF IMPORTANT ADVISORS (Cont.)

As of

_____

For more information, see page 13.

INTERVIEW QUESTIONS FOR PROSPECTIVE ADVISORS

1. *What is their specialty?*

   _____

   _____

2. *What kind of clientele do they represent?*

   _____

   _____

3. *What is their educational background?*

   _____

   _____

4. *Have they achieved any professional designations in their field?*

   _____

   _____

5. *How long have they practiced in this field?*

   _____

   _____

6. *How long have they been with this particular firm?*

   _____

   _____

7. *What professional associations do they belong to?*

   _____

   _____

8. *How large is their organization?*

   _____

   _____

INTERVIEW QUESTIONS FOR PROSPECTIVE ADVISORS (Cont.)

9. *Will they be the people who would deal with you?*

_____

_____

10. *What is the fee structure?*

_____

_____

11. *Who takes over if advisor is unavailable, out of town, or ill?*

_____

_____

12. *Will it be easy to speak to advisor when I call?*

_____

_____

13. *Would they give a home telephone number and can they be contacted there with a problem?*

_____

_____

14. _____

_____

15. _____

_____

16. _____

_____

For more information, see page 13.

ADVISOR EVALUATION GUIDE

Name of Potential Advisor: _____

Date of Interview: _____

Rating System: 1 (unsatisfactory) to 10 (excellent)

Evaluation Areas	Rating
Quality of area where office is located	_____
Educational background of advisor	_____
Work experience as it applies to my problem	_____
Size of organization	_____
Fee structure	_____
Ability to relate to me	_____
Accessibility	_____
Appearance of office	_____
Attitude of receptionist	_____
Convenience of office location	_____

TOTAL: _____

Strong points: _____

_____

Weak points: _____

_____

Additional comments: _____

_____

For more information,
see page 13.

RECORD OF ASSETS

As of

_____

Cash

Money on hand $ _____

Balance in checking account   _____

Balance in savings account   _____

Securities

Money market funds $ _____

Stock market investments   _____

Bonds   _____

U.S. Savings Bonds   _____

Mutual funds   _____

Other investments (CDs, government securities, or
repurchase agreements)   _____

Cash Surrender Value of Life Insurance Policies $ _____

Notes Receivable $ _____

Real Estate $ _____

Autos and Other Vehicles $ _____

Pension and/or Profit-Sharing Funds $ _____

Individual Retirement and Keogh Accounts $ _____

Other Assets

Home furnishings and household goods $ _____

Jewelry, furs, and silver   _____

Art and antiques   _____

Other personal property   _____

_____

RECORD
OF ASSETS
(Cont.)

As of

_____

Other items _____ _____

_____ _____

_____ _____

TOTAL ASSETS $ _____

For more information,
see page 22.

RECORD OF LIABILITIES

As of _____

Accounts Payable

Charge cards $ _____

Credit cards   _____

Medical bills and utilities   _____

Alimony and child support   _____

Other _____   _____

_____   _____

Contracts Payable

Automobiles $ _____

Furniture   _____

Installment credit contracts   _____

Notes Payable to Others

Banks $ _____

Real estate mortgages   _____

Others _____   _____

Taxes

Property taxes $ _____

Federal taxes   _____

State taxes   _____

TOTAL LIABILITIES $ _____

RECORD OF LIABILITIES (Cont.)

As of

_____

Total of Net Worth, as of _____ $_____

Assets   _____

Liabilities   −_____

Net worth   =_____

To check your figures, make sure your assets equal your liabilities plus your net worth.

For more information, see page 22.

BANKING SERVICES CHECKLIST

Services	Services Wanted	(NAME) Will Provide	(NAME) Will Provide
1. Checking Accounts			
Regular	[ ]	[ ]	[ ]
Bank by mail	[ ]	[ ]	[ ]
Drive-in teller service	[ ]	[ ]	[ ]
Check guarantee card	[ ]	[ ]	[ ]
Overdraft protection Limit: _____	[ ]	[ ]	[ ]
Market rate account	[ ]	[ ]	[ ]
Money market mutual fund	[ ]	[ ]	[ ]
2. Savings Accounts			
Passbook	[ ]	[ ]	[ ]
Trust	[ ]	[ ]	[ ]
Custodial	[ ]	[ ]	[ ]
Certificates of Deposit	[ ]	[ ]	[ ]
3. Bank Credit Card Limit: _____	[ ]	[ ]	[ ]
4. Undisbursed Loan Limit: _____	[ ]	[ ]	[ ]
5. Investment Counseling	[ ]	[ ]	[ ]
6. Trust Services	[ ]	[ ]	[ ]
7. Saturday Banking	[ ]	[ ]	[ ]
8. Banking Hours	[ ]	[ ]	[ ]
9. Loans			
Personal	[ ]	[ ]	[ ]
Home improvement	[ ]	[ ]	[ ]
Auto	[ ]	[ ]	[ ]

BANKING SERVICES CHECKLIST (Cont.)

Education	[ ]	[ ]	[ ]
Other _____	[ ]	[ ]	[ ]
10. *Safe-Deposit Box*	[ ]	[ ]	[ ]
11. *Keogh Plan*	[ ]	[ ]	[ ]
12. *Individual Retirement Accounts*	[ ]	[ ]	[ ]

For more information, see page 28.

PREPARATION CHECKLIST FOR MEETING WITH A FINANCIAL INSTITUTION

Name of institution: _____

Meeting date: _____

Target date for completion of items: _____

Item	Source of Information	Check If to Be Included	Check When Item Completed
Copy of Income Tax Returns			
19_____	_____	[ ]	[ ]
19_____	_____	[ ]	[ ]
19_____	_____	[ ]	[ ]
Financial Statement	_____	[ ]	[ ]
Budget Estimates	_____	[ ]	[ ]
Copy of Will	_____	[ ]	[ ]
Copy of Trust Agreement	_____	[ ]	[ ]
List of All Real Property	_____	[ ]	[ ]
Other	_____	[ ]	[ ]
	_____	[ ]	[ ]
	_____	[ ]	[ ]

For more information, see page 28.

INTERVIEW QUESTIONS FOR FINANCIAL INSTITUTIONS

Name:

_____

1. *How long have you been in business?*

_____

_____

2. *What are your gross assets?*

_____

_____

3. *What is the percentage of your deposits to your assets?*

_____

_____

4. *Where is your home office located?*

_____

_____

5. *How many branch offices do you have?*

_____

_____

6. *Who would be in charge of my account?*

_____

_____

7. *How long has this person worked in this office?*

_____

_____

INTERVIEW QUESTIONS FOR FINANCIAL INSTITUTIONS

Name:

_____

8. *What is that person's title?*

    _____

    _____

9. *What is that person's financial background?*

    _____

    _____

10. *What are your bank service charges or penalties?*

    _____

    _____

For more information,
see page 28.

FINANCIAL
INSTITUTION
EVALUATION
GUIDE

Name of institution: _____

Person interviewed: _____ Date _____

Rating system: 1 (unsatisfactory) to 10 (excellent)

Evaluation Areas	Rating
Appearance of branch	_____
Safety of area where located	_____
Attitude of employees	_____
Convenience of location	_____
Convenience of operating hours	_____
Reputation in the community	_____
Services available	_____
Financial stability	_____
TOTAL	_____

Strong points: _____

_____

Weak points: _____

_____

Additional comments: _____

_____

For more information,
see page 28.

COLLATERAL GUARANTEE OR CO-SIGNATURE RECORD

Effective Date	Person or Institution	Amount Involved	Type of Collateral	Due Date
————	————————	————	————————	———
————	————————	————	————————	———
————	————————	————	————————	———
————	————————	————	————————	———
————	————————	————	————————	———
————	————————	————	————————	———
————	————————	————	————————	———
————	————————	————	————————	———
————	————————	————	————————	———
————	————————	————	————————	———
————	————————	————	————————	———
————	————————	————	————————	———
————	————————	————	————————	———
————	————————	————	————————	———
————	————————	————	————————	———
————	————————	————	————————	———
————	————————	————	————————	———
————	————————	————	————————	———
————	————————	————	————————	———

For more information, see page 35.

LOAN INTEREST RATE COMPARISON

Institution	Rate of Interest				
Banks	Over-draft	Bank Card	Auto	Mortgage	Personal

Savings and Loans	Over-draft	Bank Card	Auto	Mortgage	Personal

Other	Over-draft	Bank Card	Auto	Mortgage	Personal

For more information, see page 37.

EMERGENCY CASH PLAN

Estimated Amounts

Plan arranged as of

_____

Primary Sources of Ready Cash

Extra reserve maintained in checking account $ _____

Overdraft limit in checking account   _____

Savings account   _____

Money market funds   _____

Cashable securities (stocks and bonds)   _____

Credit card limits   _____

Prearranged undisbursed loan   _____

Total ready cash from primary sources: $ _____

Secondary Sources of Immediate Cash

Borrow on cash value of life insurance policies $ _____

Borrow from credit union   _____

Borrow from profit-sharing plan   _____

Borrow from personal loan companies   _____

Secure loan on car or increase present loan   _____

Sell second car   _____

Take out second or third mortgage on home   _____

Change income tax withholding   _____

Pawn jewelry   _____

Borrow from friends and/or relatives   _____

EMERGENCY CASH PLAN (Cont.)

Estimated Amounts

Plan arranged as of

_____

Secondary Sources of Immediate Cash

Secure loan from employer _____

Emergency cash in Keogh or IRA accounts _____

Total ready cash from secondary sources: $ _____

Total potential cash from all sources: $ _____

For more information, see page 37.

DAILY CASH BUDGETING WORKSHEET

For the week of _____

Item	Monday	Tuesday	Wednesday	Thursday	Friday	Saturday	Sunday
Groceries							
Meals eaten out							
Clothing purchases							
Laundry and dry cleaning							
Entertainment (movies, plays, sporting events, toys, gifts, other)							
Health club							
Hairdresser							
Cosmetics and sundries							
Gas and oil							
Auto repairs (maintenance)							
Parking and tolls							
Public transportation							

DAILY CASH BUDGETING WORKSHEET (Cont.)

For the week of _____

	Monday	Tuesday	Wednesday	Thursday	Friday	Saturday	Sunday
School lunches							
Children's allowances							
Other _____							
TOTAL	$_____	$_____	$_____	$_____	$_____	$_____	$_____

For more information, see page 51.

MONTHLY EXPENSE BUDGETING WORKSHEET

Month of _____

List of Actual Expenses as They Occur

Item	Week 1	Week 2	Week 3	Week 4	Total Monthly Amount Spent
Housing					
Rent, condo, or mortgage payment					
Vacation home/rental property					
Property taxes					
Miscellaneous repairs					
Housekeeper					
SUBTOTAL					$
Utilities and Home Expenses					
Gas					
Electricity					
Other fuel					
Telephone					
Water and sewer					
Cable T.V.					
Garbage collection					
Gardener					
Pool maintenance					
Pest control service					
SUBTOTAL					$

MONTHLY EXPENSE BUDGETING WORKSHEET (Cont.)

Month of _____

List of Actual Expenses as They Occur

	Week 1	Week 2	Week 3	Week 4	Total Monthly Amount Spent
Personal Maintenance					
Groceries					
Meals eaten out					
Clothing purchases					
Laundry and dry cleaning					
Entertainment, including recreation and vacations					
Personal care, including health club, hairdresser, and cosmetics					
				SUBTOTAL	$
Transportation					
Gas and oil					
Repairs (maintenance)					
Parking and tolls					
License and registration					
Public transportation					
				SUBTOTAL	$

Insurance Premiums

Auto
Life
Health
Disability
Homeowners
_____
_____

SUBTOTAL $

Obligations

Installment contract payments
Furniture payments
Auto payments
Credit cards
Charge accounts
Dues and subscriptions
Taxes, federal
Taxes, state
Taxes, local

SUBTOTAL $

Child/Dependent Care

Baby-sitting fees
Nursery school fees
Special transportation
Lunches and miscellaneous items

SUBTOTAL $

Health Care

Dental visits
Doctors' visits
Drugs and vitamins

SUBTOTAL $

MONTHLY EXPENSE BUDGETING WORKSHEET (Cont.)

Month of _____

List of Actual Expenses as They Occur

Item	Week 1	Week 2	Week 3	Week 4	Total Monthly Amount Spent
Miscellaneous Expenses					
Spousal support					____
Child support					____
Education costs					____
Retirement contributions					____
Charitable contributions					____
Legal fees					____
Accountant fees					____
Children's allowances					____
Savings					____
				SUBTOTAL	$ ____

TOTAL ESTIMATED MONTHLY EXPENSES $ ____

Completed as of _____

For more information, see page 51.

ANNUAL EXPENSE BUDGETING WORKSHEET

Item	Things I Must Have	Things I Don't Need	Annual Cost	Budgeted Avg. Monthly Amount	Actual Amount Spent
Housing					
Rent, condo, or mortgage payment	[ ]	[ ]	___	___	___
Vacation home/rental property	[ ]	[ ]	___	___	___
Property taxes	[ ]	[ ]	___	___	___
Miscellaneous repairs	[ ]	[ ]	___	___	___
Housekeeper	[ ]	[ ]	___	___	___
SUBTOTAL			$___	$___	$___
Utilities and Home Expenses					
Gas	[ ]	[ ]	___	___	___
Electricity	[ ]	[ ]	___	___	___
Other fuel	[ ]	[ ]	___	___	___
Telephone	[ ]	[ ]	___	___	___
Water and sewer	[ ]	[ ]	___	___	___
Cable T.V.	[ ]	[ ]	___	___	___

ANNUAL EXPENSE BUDGETING WORKSHEET (Cont.)

Item	Things I Must Have	Things I Don't Need	Annual Cost	Budgeted Avg. Monthly Amount	Actual Amount Spent
Housing					
Garbage collection	[ ]	[ ]			
Gardener	[ ]	[ ]			
Pool maintenance	[ ]	[ ]			
Pest control services	[ ]	[ ]			
SUBTOTAL			$	$	$
Personal Maintenance					
Groceries	[ ]	[ ]			
Meals eaten out	[ ]	[ ]			
Clothing purchases	[ ]	[ ]			
Laundry and dry cleaning	[ ]	[ ]			
Entertainment, including recreation and vacations	[ ]	[ ]			
Personal care, including health club, hairdresser, and cosmetics	[ ]	[ ]			
SUBTOTAL			$	$	$

Transportation

Gas and oil

Repairs (maintenance)

Parking and tolls

License and registration

Public transportation

SUBTOTAL $

Insurance Premiums

Auto

Life

Health

Disability

Homeowners

SUBTOTAL $

Obligations

Installment contract payments

Furniture payments

Auto payments

ANNUAL EXPENSE BUDGETING WORKSHEET (Cont.)

Item	Things I Must Have	Things I Don't Need	Annual Cost	Budgeted Avg. Monthly Amount	Actual Amount Spent
Housing					
Credit cards	[ ]	[ ]	____	____	____
Charge accounts	[ ]	[ ]	____	____	____
Dues and subscriptions	[ ]	[ ]	____	____	____
Taxes, federal	[ ]	[ ]	____	____	____
Taxes, state	[ ]	[ ]	____	____	____
Taxes, local	[ ]	[ ]	____	____	____
SUBTOTAL			$ ____	$ ____	$ ____
Child/Dependent Care					
Baby-sitting fees	[ ]	[ ]	____	____	____
Nursery school fees	[ ]	[ ]	____	____	____
Special transportation	[ ]	[ ]	____	____	____
Lunches and miscellaneous items	[ ]	[ ]	____	____	____
SUBTOTAL			$ ____	$ ____	$ ____

Health Care

Dental visits [ ] [ ]

Doctors' visits [ ] [ ]

Drugs and vitamins [ ] [ ]

SUBTOTAL $ _____ $ _____ $ _____

Miscellaneous Expenses

Spousal support [ ] [ ]

Child support [ ] [ ]

Education costs [ ] [ ]

Retirement contributions [ ] [ ]

Charitable contributions [ ] [ ]

Legal fees [ ] [ ]

Accountant fees [ ] [ ]

Children's allowances [ ] [ ]

Savings [ ] [ ]

SUBTOTAL $ _____

TOTAL ESTIMATED ANNUAL EXPENSES $ _____

Completed as of _____

For more information, see page 51.

DISCRETIONARY EXPENSE WORKSHEET

Items to be Eliminated   **Monthly Amount Saved**

_____   _____

_____   _____

_____   _____

_____   _____

_____   _____

_____   _____

_____   _____

_____   _____

_____   _____

_____   _____

_____   _____

_____   _____

                        TOTAL $ _____

For more information,
see page 51.

MONTHLY BUDGET CONTROL WORKSHEET

Gross Monthly Income $ _____

Wages   _____

Salary   _____

Bonuses   _____

Real estate investments   _____

Dividends   _____

Interest   _____

Child support   _____

Alimony   _____

Other income   _____

_____   _____

_____   _____

_____   _____

TOTAL MONTHLY INCOME: _____

MONTHLY INCOME AND EXPENSE SUMMARY

Total Monthly Income: $ _____

Minus Total Monthly Expenses: – _____

Total monthly net discretionary income
available: $ _____

Discretionary expenses eliminated: _____

TOTAL MONTHLY EXPENSE BUDGET: $ _____

For more information,
see page 51.

LIST OF OWNERSHIP OF ASSETS

As of _____

Item	Type of Ownership			
	Sole and Separate Property (H or W)	Joint Tenancy	Tenants in Common	Community Property
Savings				
1. Bank _____	[ ]	[ ]	[ ]	[ ]
Acct. # _____				
2. Bank _____	[ ]	[ ]	[ ]	[ ]
Acct. # _____				
3. Bank _____	[ ]	[ ]	[ ]	[ ]
Acct. # _____				
4. Bank _____	[ ]	[ ]	[ ]	[ ]
Acct. # _____				
Checking				
1. Bank _____	[ ]	[ ]	[ ]	[ ]
Acct. # _____				
2. Bank _____	[ ]	[ ]	[ ]	[ ]
Acct. # _____				

LIST OF OWNERSHIP OF ASSETS
(Cont.)

As of _____

Item	Sole and Separate Property (H or W)	Joint Tenancy	Tenants in Common	Community Property
		Type of Ownership		
3. Bank _____	[ ]	[ ]	[ ]	[ ]
Acct. # _____				
Money Market Funds				
1. Name _____	[ ]	[ ]	[ ]	[ ]
Acct. # _____				
2. Name _____	[ ]	[ ]	[ ]	[ ]
Acct. # _____				
3. Name _____	[ ]	[ ]	[ ]	[ ]
Acct. # _____				

Stocks and Bonds

Mutual Funds

Autos and Other Vehicles

Pension Plans

LIST OF OWNERSHIP OF ASSETS (Cont.)

As of _____

Type of Ownership

Item	Sole and Separate Property (H or W)	Joint Tenancy	Tenants in Common	Community Property
IRAs and Keogh Plans				
1. Located _____	[ ]	[ ]	[ ]	[ ]
Acct. # _____	[ ]	[ ]	[ ]	[ ]
2. Located _____				
Acct. # _____				
Limited Partnerships				
_____	[ ]	[ ]	[ ]	[ ]
_____	[ ]	[ ]	[ ]	[ ]
Real Estate				
_____	[ ]	[ ]	[ ]	[ ]
_____	[ ]	[ ]	[ ]	[ ]

For more information, see page 56.

ESTATE PLANNING CHECKLIST

Item	Source of Information	Needed for Meeting	Target Date to Have Ready	Information Completed for Meeting
Income Tax Returns				
19___	_____	[ ]	_____	[ ]
19___	_____	[ ]	_____	[ ]
19___	_____	[ ]	_____	[ ]
Financial Statement	(see Chap. 3)	[ ]	_____	[ ]
List of Real Estate	(see Chap. 1)	[ ]	_____	[ ]
Copy of Current Will	_____	[ ]	_____	[ ]
Ownership of Assets Worksheet	(see Worksheet #28)	[ ]	_____	[ ]
Life Insurance Policies	(see Chap. 1)	[ ]	_____	[ ]
Will Preparation Worksheet	(see Chap. 9)	[ ]	_____	[ ]

For more information, see page 56.

WILL PREPARATION WORKSHEET

Names of Beneficiaries
(Family, Friends, Charitable Institutions)

Relationship

Bequest
(Percentage of Estate, Cash Amount, or Article)

1.

2.

3.

4.

5.

6.

7.

8.

9.

10.

11.

12.

WILL PREPARATION WORKSHEET (Cont.)

Executor: *First Choice* _____

Successor _____

Trustee: *First Choice* _____

Successor or Alternate _____

For more information, see page 61.

WHEN TO REVIEW A WILL

	Check If Reviewed	Date

Family Relations

Separation or dissolution of marriage _____ _____

Severe illness, death, incapacity, or death of a spouse _____ _____

New grandchild _____ _____

Economic and Personal Conditions

Significant financial gains or reversals _____ _____

Acquisition of property in a different state _____ _____

Change in life insurance insurability _____ _____

Change in employment _____ _____

Change in business interests: sale, purchase, incorporation, and/or dissolution of business _____ _____

Change in health _____ _____

Retirement _____ _____

External Changes

Change in laws: state and federal income, estate, and gift tax laws; state property, trust, and probate laws _____ _____

Change of residence to another state _____ _____

Death, illness of the executor, trustee, guardian, or conservator to serve _____ _____

For more information, see page 62.

EVALUATION GUIDE: INDIVIDUAL EXECUTOR OR TRUSTEE

Name of Nominee: _____

Review Date: _____

Rating System: 1 (unsatisfactory) to 10 (excellent)

Evaluation Areas	Rating
General business knowledge	_____
General knowledge of family situation	_____
Reputation	_____
Stability	_____
Maturity	_____
Time available	_____
Health	_____
Fiscal soundness	_____
Other _____	_____
_____	_____
_____	_____
TOTAL	_____

Strong points: _____

_____

Weak points: _____

_____

Additional comments: _____

_____

For more information,
see page 63.

EVALUATION GUIDE INSTITUTIONAL EXECUTOR OR TRUSTEE

Name of Nominee: _____

Review Date: _____

Rating System: 1 (unsatisfactory) to 10 (excellent)

Evaluation Areas	Rating
Experience	_____
Reputation	_____
Educational background of employees	_____
Size of organization	_____
Quality of person with whom you deal	_____
General attitude	_____
Fiscal soundness	_____
Other _____	_____
_____	_____
_____	_____
TOTAL	_____

Strong points: _____
_____

Weak points: _____
_____

Additional comments: _____
_____

For more information,
see page 64.

EVALUATION GUIDE: GUARDIAN OF THE PERSON

Name of Potential Guardian: _____

Review Date: _____

Rating System: 1 (unsatisfactory) to 10 (excellent)

Evaluation Areas	Rating
Maturity and experience	_____
Temperament	_____
Stamina	_____
Integrity	_____
Stability	_____
Home environment	_____
Financial resources	_____
Ability to relate to your children	_____
Health	_____
Others _____	_____
_____	_____
_____	_____
TOTAL	_____

Strong points: _____

_____

Weak points: _____

_____

Additional comments: _____

_____

For more information, see page 68.

EVALUATION GUIDE: GUARDIAN OF THE ESTATE

Name of Potential Guardian: _____

Review Date: _____

Rating System: 1 (unsatisfactory) to 10 (excellent)

Evaluation Areas	Rating
Financial knowledge	_____
General business background	_____
Fee structure	_____
Maturity and experience	_____
Integrity	_____
Stability	_____
Ability to relate to your children	_____
Health	_____
Others _____	_____
_____	_____
_____	_____
TOTAL	_____

Strong points: _____

_____

Weak points: _____

_____

Additional comments: _____

_____

For more information, see page 68.

TRUSTEE EVALUATION GUIDE

Name of Potential Trustee: _____

Review Date: _____

Rating System: 1 (unsatisfactory) to 10 (excellent)

Evaluation Areas	Rating
Financial knowledge	_____
Maturity and experience	_____
Stability	_____
Integrity	_____
Business background	_____
Fee structure	_____
Ability to relate to your children	_____
Health	_____
TOTAL	_____

Strong points: _____

_____

Weak points: _____

_____

Additional comments: _____

_____

For more information,
see page 69.

CHILDPROOF PROTECTION SUMMARY

Primary Guardian: _____

Secondary Guardian: _____

Primary Trustee: _____

Secondary Trustee: _____

Date of Current Will: _____

*Review of Will
and Tax Provisions:* _____

_____

_____

Child's Name	Distribution of Funds (% or $ Amounts)					
	Age	Amt.	Age	Amt.	Age	Amt.
_____	____	____	____	____	____	____
_____	____	____	____	____	____	____
_____	____	____	____	____	____	____
_____	____	____	____	____	____	____

Special Provision Reminders

1. Is there provision for emergency medical treatment?
2. Is there flexibility for other emergency funds?
3. Is there an adequate allotment for guardians?
4. Has a health problem developed requiring new provisions?
5. Have tax laws recently changed?

For more information,
see page 70.

LIFE INSURANCE WORKSHEET

Immediate Cash Needs	Amount
Pay off debts	$ _____
Pay medical bills *(Not covered by insurance)*	_____
Emergency funds needed	_____
Federal or state estate taxes	_____
Other _____	_____
TOTAL	$ _____

Monthly Cash Needs	
Continuing monthly expenses	$ _____
Replace loss of income	_____
Income for dependents	_____
Additional housekeeping expenses	_____
Other _____	_____
TOTAL	$ _____

Long-Term Cash Needs	
Savings	$ _____
Retirement	_____
College funds	_____
Lump-sum payments to dependents	_____
Other _____	_____
TOTAL	$ _____

LIFE INSURANCE WORKSHEET (Cont.)

Summary of Cash Needs

Immediate Cash $ _____

Monthly cash
a. Multiply monthly income by 12 to get annual needs
b. Multiply annual by number of years you want to
   provide   _____

Long-term cash   _____

                              TOTAL CASH NEEDS $ _____

Value of Other Assets $ _____
(see Worksheets #s14–19)

Life Insurance Needs $ _____
(Cash needs less assets)

For more information,
see page 71.

DEPENDENT INCOME WORKSHEET

Monthly Income

Dependent	Monthly Amount	Number of Years	
	$		

TOTAL $_____

Lump Sum Payments

Dependent	Amount

DEPENDENT INCOME WORKSHEET (Cont.)

Monthly Income

_____ _____

_____ _____

_____ _____

TOTAL $_____

For more information,
see page 74.

BENEFICIARY WORKSHEET

Name	Relationship	Total Amount of Money I Want Them to Have	Specific Assets I Want Them to Have

For more information, see page 74.

Comprehensive Medical Care

Deductible: Per Individual _____ *Per Family* _____

Calendar Year _____ *Per Condition* _____

Maximum Limit _____

Basic Surgical

Maximum Limit _____

Surgical Schedule: _____

_____ *Reasonable and Customary*

_____ *Relative Value Schedule*

_____ *Specific Limits*

_____ *In or Out of Hospital*

_____ *Doctor's Office*

Basic Hospital

Daily Limit _____

Number of Days _____

Maximum Limit _____

Deductible: Per Individual _____ *Per Family* _____

Calendar Year _____ *Per Condition* _____

*Miscellaneous Hospital
Expense Limit* _____

Hospital Confinement

Deductible _____

Daily Limit _____

Maximum Limit _____

MEDICAL INSURANCE COVERAGE WORKSHEET (Cont.)

Major Medical

Maximum Limit _____

Deductible: Per Individual _____ Per Family _____

Calendar Year _____ Per Condition _____

Excess Major Medical

Maximum _____

Deductible: Per Individual _____ Per Family _____

Calendar Year _____ Per Condition _____

Special Clauses—Does your policy include:

	Yes	No
Pre-existing condition	[ ]	[ ]
Dependents		
a. Until age ____	[ ]	[ ]
b. Residing at home	[ ]	[ ]
Nursing care	[ ]	[ ]
Home care (nurses and therapists)	[ ]	[ ]
Nursing homes	[ ]	[ ]
Maternity benefits	[ ]	[ ]
Prevailing rate clause	[ ]	[ ]
Second-opinion surgery	[ ]	[ ]
30-day conversion clause	[ ]	[ ]
Noncancelable clause	[ ]	[ ]
Guaranteed renewable	[ ]	[ ]
Hospital pre-authorization clause	[ ]	[ ]

MEDICAL INSURANCE COVERAGE WORKSHEET (Cont.)

Special Clauses—Does your policy include: Yes   No

Psychological coverage   [ ]   [ ]

Spousal conversion   [ ]   [ ]

Accidental death   [ ]   [ ]

Life insurance   [ ]   [ ]

For more information, see page 86.

MEDICAL INSURANCE COST/COVERAGE COMPARISON

Type of Coverage

	Insurance Co. No. 1		Insurance Co. No. 2	
	Premium	Coverage	Premium	Coverage
Basic Medical Expense	$ _____	_____	$ _____	_____
Maximum Limit	_____	_____	_____	_____
Deductible	_____	_____	_____	_____
Basic Surgical Expense	$ _____	_____	$ _____	_____
Maximum Limit	_____	_____	_____	_____
Deductible	_____	_____	_____	_____
Basic Hospital Expense	$ _____	_____	$ _____	_____
Daily Limit	_____	_____	_____	_____
Number of Days	_____	_____	_____	_____
Maximum Limit	_____	_____	_____	_____
Deductible	_____	_____	_____	_____

MEDICAL INSURANCE COST/COVERAGE COMPARISON (Cont.)

Type of Coverage	Insurance Co. No. 1		Insurance Co. No. 2	
	Premium	Coverage	Premium	Coverage
Hospital Confinement	$ _____	_____	$ _____	_____
Daily Limit	_____	_____	_____	_____
Maximum Limit	_____	_____	_____	_____
Deductible	_____	_____	_____	_____
Major Medical	$ _____	_____	$ _____	_____
Limit	_____	_____	_____	_____
Deductible	_____	_____	_____	_____
Excess Major Medical	$ _____	_____	$ _____	_____
Limit	_____	_____	_____	_____
Deductible	_____	_____	_____	_____
Medicare Supplement	$ _____	_____	$ _____	_____
Amount	_____	_____	_____	_____

MEDICAL INSURANCE COST/COVERAGE COMPARISON (Cont.)

For more information, see page 86.

Accident Only $ _____ $ _____

Amount _____ _____

Specific Diseases $ _____ $ _____

Amount $ _____ $ _____

Remarks: _____

_____

_____

EVALUATING HMO AND GROUP INSURANCE

Potential Health Maintenance Organization: _____

Potential Insurance Company: _____

Rating: 1 (unsatisfactory) to 10 (excellent)

Evaluation Areas	HMO	Insurance Company
Basic hospital coverage	_____	_____
Basic surgical coverage	_____	_____
Coverage deductible	_____	_____
Training of physicians in general	_____	_____
Ability of physicians to relate to you	_____	_____
Convenience of location	_____	_____
Quality of area where located	_____	_____
Size of company	_____	_____
Appearance of office	_____	_____
Outside local area benefits	_____	_____
TOTALS	_____	_____

EVALUATING HMO AND GROUP INSURANCE (Cont.)

	HMO	Insurance Company
General comments:	_____	_____
	_____	_____
	_____	_____
	_____	_____
	_____	_____
	_____	_____
Strong points:	_____	_____
	_____	_____
	_____	_____
	_____	_____
	_____	_____
Weak points:	_____	_____
	_____	_____
	_____	_____
	_____	_____
	_____	_____

For more information, see page 87.

DISABILITY INSURANCE CHECKLIST

	Yes	No

1. *How does policy define disability:*

   a. *Can you perform your particular job?*   [ ]   [ ]

   b. *Can you work at any occupation?*   [ ]   [ ]

   c. *Would you lose money if you worked part-time?*   [ ]   [ ]

   d. *Must you be totally hospitalized for benefits?*   [ ]   [ ]

   e. *Must you be totally house-bound for benefits?*   [ ]   [ ]

   f. *Other* _____   [ ]   [ ]

2. *Is the policy guaranteed renewable?*   [ ]   [ ]

3. *Is there a waiting period before payments begin?*   [ ]   [ ]

4. *Is there an employment eligibility period?*   [ ]   [ ]

5. *Is there a "survivor" benefit?*   [ ]   [ ]

6. *Is there a mental illness exclusion?*   [ ]   [ ]

7. *Must you pay premiums while receiving disability payments?*   [ ]   [ ]

8. *Is there a rehabilitative benefit?*   [ ]   [ ]

9. *Are benefits reduced if you have other sources of income?*   [ ]   [ ]

   Earned [ ]   *Unearned* [ ]   *Social Security* [ ]
   Workers Compensation [ ]

10. *What is the elimination period?*
    30 days [ ]   *60 days* [ ]   *90 days* [ ]   *Over 90 days* [ ]

11. *Benefits are based on:*

    a. *Length of service* [ ] _____

    b. *Salary*   [ ] _____

DISABILITY INSURANCE CHECKLIST (Cont.)

12. *How long do the payments last?*

    a. For sickness: _____

    b. For accident: _____

    c. What are the total monthly benefits? _____

    d. What is the maximum benefit payable? _____

For more information,
see page 91.

EMERGENCY DISABILITY PLAN

Plan arranged as of

_____

I. Ready Cash   Estimated Amounts

   A. Primary sources

     1. Disability insurance $_____

     2. Social Security or state disability benefits   _____

     3. Money market funds   _____

     4. Savings account   _____

     5. Cashable securities (stocks and bonds)   _____

     6. Bank loans (pre-arranged)   _____

     7. Regular checking account   _____

     8. Checking account overdraft protection   _____

     9. Credit card limits   _____

         Cash from primary sources $_____

   B. Secondary sources

     1. Borrow on the cash value of life insurance policies $_____

     2. Borrow from profit-sharing plan   _____

     3. Borrow from credit union   _____

     4. Borrow from personal loan companies   _____

     5. Secure loan on the car or increase present loan   _____

     6. Secure cash from Keogh or IRA account   _____

EMERGENCY DISABILITY PLAN (Cont.)

Plan arranged as of

_____

I. <u>Ready Cash</u>   Estimated Amounts

    7. _Take out a second or third mortgage on the home_ _____

    8. _Notify employer to change your federal withholding_ _____

    9. _Creditor loans_ _____

    10. _Pawn jewelry_ _____

    11. _Sell collections_ _____

    12. _Borrow from friends or relatives_ _____

    13. _Secure loan from employer_ _____

    14. _Sell second car_ _____

    15. _Other_ _____ _____

Cash from secondary sources $_____

TOTAL READY CASH $_____

II. <u>Expenses</u>   Monthly Amount

    A. _New Expenses_

        1. _Medical costs_

            a. Hospital costs not covered by insurance $_____

            b. Doctors' fees not covered by insurance _____

            c. Private nursing _____

            d. Drugs and miscellaneous _____

II. Expenses   Monthly Amount

EMERGENCY
DISABILITY
PLAN
(Cont.)

Plan arranged as of

   2. *Other expenses*

     a. Transportation   _____ _____

     b. House expenses   _____

        1. New household maintenance expenses _____

        2. Extra baby-sitting because of your absence _____

     c. Others

        1. _____ _____

        2. _____ _____

        3. _____ _____

        4. _____ _____

B. *Regular Monthly Expenses (from budget)* _____

TOTAL MONTHLY EXPENSES $_____

III. Emergency Action Plans During This Period

   A. *List all expenses you can reduce during this period:*

     1. _____

     2. _____

     3. _____

     4. _____

     5. _____

EMERGENCY DISABILITY PLAN (Cont.)

Plan arranged as of

_____

III. Emergency Action Plans During This Period

    B. *List all creditors who would extend payment period:*

       1. _____

       2. _____

       3. _____

       4. _____

       5. _____

    C. *Notify the disability insurance company to begin benefits.*

    D. *Recheck your medical insurance so you know exactly what the deductibles and coverages are.*

    E. *Determine which friends, relatives, and neighbors will assist you with certain functions.*

    F. *Notify the children's schools of problems at home.*

    G. *Contact community support groups, such as United Way, for information regarding assistance with transportation, visiting nurses, etc.*

    H. _____

    I. _____

    J. _____

    K. _____

For more information, see page 93.

LONG-TERM DISABILITY PLAN

As of _____

1. Sources of Income   Estimated Amounts
_____

    A.   *Monthly income from disability insurance* $_____

    B.   *Monthly income from 90-day emergency plan* $_____

    C.   *Other sources of monthly income*

      _____ _____

      _____ _____

      _____ _____

              TOTAL MONTHLY INCOME $_____

              TOTAL AUSTERITY BUDGET $_____

              CASH NEEDS $_____

2. Pre-arranged Expense Reduction   Amount of Decrease
_____

    1.   _____ $_____

    2.   _____ _____

    3.   _____ _____

    4.   _____ _____

    5.   _____ _____

    6.   _____ _____

    7.   _____ _____

    8.   _____ _____

       TOTAL MONTHLY AUSTERITY BUDGET $_____

            TOTAL MONTHLY INCOME $_____

         TOTAL MONTHLY CASH NEEDS $_____

LONG-TERM DISABILITY PLAN
(Cont.)

As of

_____

3. Potential Income Sources   Estimated Amounts
    _____

    A. *Wife works full or part-time* $_____

    B. *Children work part-time*   _____

    C. *Establish a home business*   _____

    D. _____   _____

    E. _____   _____

    F. _____   _____

    G. _____   _____

                                        TOTAL **$**_____

For more information, see page 94.

HOUSEHOLD INVENTORY RECORD

Completed as of

_____

Living Room

Item	Qty.	Cost New	Current Value	Total Value
Books and Bookcases (portable)	_____	[ ]	[ ]	_____
Chairs	_____	[ ]	[ ]	_____
Clocks	_____	[ ]	[ ]	_____
Couches, Divans, Sofas	_____	[ ]	[ ]	_____
Desks and Desk Accessories	_____	[ ]	[ ]	_____
Drapes, Curtains, and Blinds	_____	[ ]	[ ]	_____
Fine Arts	_____	[ ]	[ ]	_____
Fireplace Fixtures	_____	[ ]	[ ]	_____
Floor Lamps	_____	[ ]	[ ]	_____
Hi-Fi (stereo)	_____	[ ]	[ ]	_____
Lamps	_____	[ ]	[ ]	_____
Mirrors (portable)	_____	[ ]	[ ]	_____
Musical Instruments	_____	[ ]	[ ]	_____
Phonograph Records and Tapes	_____	[ ]	[ ]	_____
Pictures	_____	[ ]	[ ]	_____
Pillows and Cushions	_____	[ ]	[ ]	_____
Planters	_____	[ ]	[ ]	_____
Radio	_____	[ ]	[ ]	_____
Rugs and Carpets (not attached)	_____	[ ]	[ ]	_____

HOUSEHOLD INVENTORY RECORD

Living Room

Item	Qty.	Cost New	Current Value	Total Value
Shelves and Wall Units	_____	[ ]	[ ]	_____
Tables and Table Accessories	_____	[ ]	[ ]	_____
Television	_____	[ ]	[ ]	_____
_____	_____	[ ]	[ ]	_____
_____	_____	[ ]	[ ]	_____
_____	_____	[ ]	[ ]	_____
_____	_____	[ ]	[ ]	_____
_____	_____	[ ]	[ ]	_____
_____	_____	[ ]	[ ]	_____

HOUSEHOLD INVENTORY RECORD

Dining Room and Dinette

Item	Qty.	Cost New	Current Value	Total Value
Benches	_____	[ ]	[ ]	_____
Buffet	_____	[ ]	[ ]	_____
Candlesticks	_____	[ ]	[ ]	_____
Carts	_____	[ ]	[ ]	_____
Chairs	_____	[ ]	[ ]	_____
Chests	_____	[ ]	[ ]	_____
China Cabinet	_____	[ ]	[ ]	_____
China and Glassware	_____	[ ]	[ ]	_____
Clocks	_____	[ ]	[ ]	_____
Drapes, Curtains, and Blinds	_____	[ ]	[ ]	_____
Electric Utensils	_____	[ ]	[ ]	_____
Fine Arts	_____	[ ]	[ ]	_____
Glasses	_____	[ ]	[ ]	_____
Linens	_____	[ ]	[ ]	_____
Mirrors (portable)	_____	[ ]	[ ]	_____
Pictures	_____	[ ]	[ ]	_____
Rugs and Carpets (not attached)	_____	[ ]	[ ]	_____
Serving Tables	_____	[ ]	[ ]	_____
Silverware	_____	[ ]	[ ]	_____
Table and Chairs	_____	[ ]	[ ]	_____
Table Linen	_____	[ ]	[ ]	_____
_____	_____	[ ]	[ ]	_____

HOUSEHOLD INVENTORY RECORD

Bedrooms

Item	Qty. (Master Bdrm.)	Value (Master Bdrm.)	Qty. (Second Bdrm.)	Value (Second Bdrm.)
Beds	_____	_____	_____	_____
Bedspreads, Sheets, Blankets, and Quilts	_____	_____	_____	_____
Chairs	_____	_____	_____	_____
Chaise Longues	_____	_____	_____	_____
Clocks	_____	_____	_____	_____
Clothing	_____	_____	_____	_____
Cosmetics	_____	_____	_____	_____
Drapes, Curtains, and Blinds	_____	_____	_____	_____
Dressers and Chests	_____	_____	_____	_____
Dressing Tables	_____	_____	_____	_____
Fine Arts	_____	_____	_____	_____
Hi-Fi (stereo)	_____	_____	_____	_____
Lamps	_____	_____	_____	_____
Mattress/Box Springs	_____	_____	_____	_____
Mirrors (portable)	_____	_____	_____	_____
Pictures	_____	_____	_____	_____
Radio	_____	_____	_____	_____
Rugs and Carpets (not attached)	_____	_____	_____	_____
Tables and Nightstands	_____	_____	_____	_____
Television	_____	_____	_____	_____

Qty. (Third Bdrm.)	Value	Qty. (Fourth Bdrm.)	Value	Cost New	Current Value	Total Value
____	____	____	____	[	] [	] ____
____	____	____	____	[	] [	] ____
____	____	____	____	[	] [	] ____
____	____	____	____	[	] [	] ____
____	____	____	____	[	] [	] ____
____	____	____	____	[	] [	] ____
____	____	____	____	[	] [	] ____
____	____	____	____	[	] [	] ____
____	____	____	____	[	] [	] ____
____	____	____	____	[	] [	] ____
____	____	____	____	[	] [	] ____
____	____	____	____	[	] [	] ____
____	____	____	____	[	] [	] ____
____	____	____	____	[	] [	] ____
____	____	____	____	[	] [	] ____
____	____	____	____	[	] [	] ____
____	____	____	____	[	] [	] ____
____	____	____	____	[	] [	] ____
____	____	____	____	[	] [	] ____

HOUSEHOLD INVENTORY RECORD

Bedrooms

Item	Qty. (Master Bdrm.)	Value	Qty. (Second Bdrm.)	Value
	_____	_____	_____	_____
	_____	_____	_____	_____
	_____	_____	_____	_____
	_____	_____	_____	_____
	_____	_____	_____	_____
	_____	_____	_____	_____

SUBTOTAL $_____   SUBTOTAL $_____

Qty. (Third Bdrm.)	Value	Qty. (Fourth Bdrm.)	Value	Cost New	Current Value	Total Value
___	___	___	___	[ ]	[ ]	___
___	___	___	___	[ ]	[ ]	___
___	___	___	___	[ ]	[ ]	___
___	___	___	___	[ ]	[ ]	___
___	___	___	___	[ ]	[ ]	___
___	___	___	___	[ ]	[ ]	___

SUBTOTAL $_____   **SUBTOTAL $**_____   **TOTAL $**_____

HOUSEHOLD INVENTORY RECORD

Bathrooms

Item	Qty.	Cost New	Current Value	Total Value
Clothes Hampers	_____	[　　]	[　　]	_____
Curtains	_____	[　　]	[　　]	_____
Dressing Tables	_____	[　　]	[　　]	_____
Electric Curlers	_____	[　　]	[　　]	_____
Hair Dryers and Curling Irons	_____	[　　]	[　　]	_____
Linens	_____	[　　]	[　　]	_____
Medicines and Drugs	_____	[　　]	[　　]	_____
Mirrors (portable)	_____	[　　]	[　　]	_____
Perfumes and Toiletries	_____	[　　]	[　　]	_____
Rugs (unattached)	_____	[　　]	[　　]	_____
Scales	_____	[　　]	[　　]	_____
Shaving Equipment	_____	[　　]	[　　]	_____
Shower Curtains	_____	[　　]	[　　]	_____
Sun Lamps	_____	[　　]	[　　]	_____
Towels	_____	[　　]	[　　]	_____
Wall Hangings	_____	[　　]	[　　]	_____
_____	_____	[　　]	[　　]	_____
_____	_____	[　　]	[　　]	_____
_____	_____	[　　]	[　　]	_____
_____	_____	[　　]	[　　]	_____

HOUSEHOLD INVENTORY RECORD

Kitchen and Pantry

Item	Qty.	Cost New	Current Value	Total Value
Blender and Toaster	_____	[ ]	[ ]	_____
Canned Goods and Staples	_____	[ ]	[ ]	_____
Cleaning Materials	_____	[ ]	[ ]	_____
Clocks	_____	[ ]	[ ]	_____
Coffee Maker and Mixer	_____	[ ]	[ ]	_____
Cookware—Pots and Pans	_____	[ ]	[ ]	_____
Curtains and Blinds	_____	[ ]	[ ]	_____
Cutlery	_____	[ ]	[ ]	_____
Dishes	_____	[ ]	[ ]	_____
Dishwasher	_____	[ ]	[ ]	_____
Freezer	_____	[ ]	[ ]	_____
Glassware	_____	[ ]	[ ]	_____
Liquor and Wines	_____	[ ]	[ ]	_____
Microwave Oven—Oven	_____	[ ]	[ ]	_____
Radio and Television	_____	[ ]	[ ]	_____
Refrigerator	_____	[ ]	[ ]	_____
Tables and Chairs	_____	[ ]	[ ]	_____
Waxer-Buffer	_____	[ ]	[ ]	_____
_____	_____	[ ]	[ ]	_____
_____	_____	[ ]	[ ]	_____
_____		[ ]	[ ]	_____

HOUSEHOLD INVENTORY RECORD

Family Room or Den

Item	Qty.	Cost New	Current Value	Total Value
Books and Bookcases (portable)	_____	[ ]	[ ]	_____
Chairs and Cabinets	_____	[ ]	[ ]	_____
Clocks	_____	[ ]	[ ]	_____
Computer	_____	[ ]	[ ]	_____
Couches, Divans, and Sofas	_____	[ ]	[ ]	_____
Desks and Accessories	_____	[ ]	[ ]	_____
Drapes, Curtains, and Blinds	_____	[ ]	[ ]	_____
Fine Arts	_____	[ ]	[ ]	_____
Fireplace Fixtures	_____	[ ]	[ ]	_____
Game Sets	_____	[ ]	[ ]	_____
Hi-Fi (stereo) and Radios	_____	[ ]	[ ]	_____
Lamps	_____	[ ]	[ ]	_____
Mirrors (portable)	_____	[ ]	[ ]	_____
Musical Instruments	_____	[ ]	[ ]	_____
Phonograph Records and Tapes	_____	[ ]	[ ]	_____
Pictures	_____	[ ]	[ ]	_____
Pillows and Cushions	_____	[ ]	[ ]	_____
Planters	_____	[ ]	[ ]	_____
Rugs and Carpets (not attached)	_____	[ ]	[ ]	_____

HOUSEHOLD INVENTORY RECORD

Family Room or Den

Item	Qty.	Cost New	Current Value	Total Value
Tables and Accessories	———	[ ]	[ ]	———
Television	———	[ ]	[ ]	———
Video Recorder and Tapes	———	[ ]	[ ]	———
———————————	———	[ ]	[ ]	———
———————————	———	[ ]	[ ]	———
———————————	———	[ ]	[ ]	———
———————————	———	[ ]	[ ]	———
———————————	———	[ ]	[ ]	———
———————————	———	[ ]	[ ]	———

HOUSEHOLD INVENTORY RECORD

Appliances, Equipment, and Miscellaneous Items

Item	Qty.	Cost New	Current Value	Total Value
Air Conditioner	_____	[ ]	[ ]	_____
De-Humidifier or Humidifier	_____	[ ]	[ ]	_____
Dryer	_____	[ ]	[ ]	_____
Exercise Equipment	_____	[ ]	[ ]	_____
Fans	_____	[ ]	[ ]	_____
Heaters	_____	[ ]	[ ]	_____
Sewing Machine	_____	[ ]	[ ]	_____
Sporting Equipment	_____	[ ]	[ ]	_____
Tools—Power and Hand	_____	[ ]	[ ]	_____
Vacuum Cleaners	_____	[ ]	[ ]	_____
Washers	_____	[ ]	[ ]	_____
Workbenches	_____	[ ]	[ ]	_____
Yard Supplies— Garden Tools	_____	[ ]	[ ]	_____
_____	_____	[ ]	[ ]	_____
_____	_____	[ ]	[ ]	_____
_____	_____	[ ]	[ ]	_____
_____	_____	[ ]	[ ]	_____
_____	_____	[ ]	[ ]	_____
_____	_____	[ ]	[ ]	_____
_____	_____	[ ]	[ ]	_____
_____	_____	[ ]	[ ]	_____

HOUSEHOLD INVENTORY RECORD

Your Personal Belongings

Item	Qty.	Cost New	Current Value	Total Value
Beachwear	_____	[ ]	[ ]	_____
Belts	_____	[ ]	[ ]	_____
Blouses	_____	[ ]	[ ]	_____
Boots	_____	[ ]	[ ]	_____
Raincoats, Coats, and Jackets	_____	[ ]	[ ]	_____
Dresses	_____	[ ]	[ ]	_____
Furs	_____	[ ]	[ ]	_____
Gloves, Handkerchiefs, and Scarves	_____	[ ]	[ ]	_____
Gowns	_____	[ ]	[ ]	_____
Handbags	_____	[ ]	[ ]	_____
Hats	_____	[ ]	[ ]	_____
Jeans	_____	[ ]	[ ]	_____
Jewelry	_____	[ ]	[ ]	_____
Lingerie and Robes	_____	[ ]	[ ]	_____
Luggage	_____	[ ]	[ ]	_____
Pants	_____	[ ]	[ ]	_____
Shoes	_____	[ ]	[ ]	_____
Skirts	_____	[ ]	[ ]	_____
Sleepwear	_____	[ ]	[ ]	_____
Suits	_____	[ ]	[ ]	_____
Sweaters	_____	[ ]	[ ]	_____

HOUSEHOLD INVENTORY RECORD

Husband's Personal Belongings

Item	Qty.	Cost New	Current Value	Total Value
Beachwear	_____	[ ]	[ ]	_____
Belts	_____	[ ]	[ ]	_____
Coats	_____	[ ]	[ ]	_____
Formal Wear	_____	[ ]	[ ]	_____
Gloves and Handkerchiefs	_____	[ ]	[ ]	_____
Hats	_____	[ ]	[ ]	_____
Jeans	_____	[ ]	[ ]	_____
Luggage	_____	[ ]	[ ]	_____
Overcoats and Raincoats	_____	[ ]	[ ]	_____
Pajamas	_____	[ ]	[ ]	_____
Robes	_____	[ ]	[ ]	_____
Shirts	_____	[ ]	[ ]	_____
Shoes	_____	[ ]	[ ]	_____
Slacks	_____	[ ]	[ ]	_____
Socks	_____	[ ]	[ ]	_____
Sport Jackets	_____	[ ]	[ ]	_____
Suits	_____	[ ]	[ ]	_____
Suspenders	_____	[ ]	[ ]	_____
Sweaters	_____	[ ]	[ ]	_____
Ties	_____	[ ]	[ ]	_____
_____	_____	[ ]	[ ]	_____
_____	_____	[ ]	[ ]	_____

HOUSEHOLD INVENTORY RECORD

Children's Clothing

Item	Qty.	Cost New	Current Value	Total Value
Beachwear	———	[ ]	[ ]	———
Blouses	———	[ ]	[ ]	———
Coats, Raincoats, and Jackets	———	[ ]	[ ]	———
Dresses	———	[ ]	[ ]	———
Gloves, Mittens, and Belts	———	[ ]	[ ]	———
Handkerchiefs	———	[ ]	[ ]	———
Hats, Caps, and Purses	———	[ ]	[ ]	———
Jeans	———	[ ]	[ ]	———
Jewelry	———	[ ]	[ ]	———
Luggage	———	[ ]	[ ]	———
Shirts	———	[ ]	[ ]	———
Shoes and Boots	———	[ ]	[ ]	———
Slacks	———	[ ]	[ ]	———
Sleepwear and Robes	———	[ ]	[ ]	———
Suits	———	[ ]	[ ]	———
Sweaters	———	[ ]	[ ]	———
Ties	———	[ ]	[ ]	———
———————	———	[ ]	[ ]	———
———————	———	[ ]	[ ]	———
———————	———	[ ]	[ ]	———
		[ ]	[ ]	———

For more information, see page 97.

SPECIAL INVENTORY: RECORD OF JEWELRY, SILVERWARE, ART

Item	Qty.	Cost New	Current Value	Total Value
JEWELRY	————	[　　]	[　　]	————
Bracelets	————	[　　]	[　　]	————
Buckles and Clips	————	[　　]	[　　]	————
Cuff Links	————	[　　]	[　　]	————
Earrings	————	[　　]	[　　]	————
Necklaces	————	[　　]	[　　]	————
Pins and Brooches	————	[　　]	[　　]	————
Rings	————	[　　]	[　　]	————
Stickpins and Studs	————	[　　]	[　　]	————
Watches	————	[　　]	[　　]	————
————————	————	[　　]	[　　]	————
SILVERWARE OR FLATWARE (List major items)				
————————	————	[　　]	[　　]	————
————————	————	[　　]	[　　]	————
————————	————	[　　]	[　　]	————
ART WORKS				
————————	————	[　　]	[　　]	————
————————	————	[　　]	[　　]	————
COLLECTIBLES				
————————	————	[　　]	[　　]	————
————————	————	[　　]	[　　]	————
————————	————	[　　]	[　　]	————

SPECIAL INVENTORY: RECORD OF JEWELRY, SILVERWARE, ART

Item	Qty.	Cost New	Current Value	Total Value

OTHER

Item	Qty.	Cost New	Current Value	Total Value
_____	____	[ ]	[ ]	_____
_____	____	[ ]	[ ]	_____
_____	____	[ ]	[ ]	_____
_____	____	[ ]	[ ]	_____
_____	____	[ ]	[ ]	_____
_____	____	[ ]	[ ]	_____
_____	____	[ ]	[ ]	_____
_____	____	[ ]	[ ]	_____
_____	____	[ ]	[ ]	_____
_____	____	[ ]	[ ]	_____
_____	____	[ ]	[ ]	_____
_____	____	[ ]	[ ]	_____
_____	____	[ ]	[ ]	_____
_____	____	[ ]	[ ]	_____
_____	____	[ ]	[ ]	_____
_____	____	[ ]	[ ]	_____
_____	____	[ ]	[ ]	_____
_____	____	[ ]	[ ]	_____
_____	____	[ ]	[ ]	_____
_____	____	[ ]	[ ]	_____
_____	____	[ ]	[ ]	_____
_____	____	[ ]	[ ]	_____

For more information, see page 97.

HOMEOWNERS INSURANCE CHECKLIST

As of _____

	Insured	Amount

1. Home

A. House valued at replacement cost
of _____   [ ] $_____

Value determined by:
    Insurance broker   ( )
    General contractor   ( )
    Real estate broker   ( )

Cost per square foot
    Number of square feet _____
    multiplied by cost of _____

B. Special coverage for earthquake   [ ]   _____

Special coverage for flood damage   [ ]   _____

Other _____   [ ]   _____

2. Detached Structures

A. Garages   [ ] $_____

B. Pool houses   [ ]   _____

C. Tool storage   [ ]   _____

D. Guest houses   [ ]   _____

E. Other _____   [ ]   _____

3. Contents of Home, Apartment, or Condominium

Contents insured for:
    Depreciated value   [ ] $_____
    Replacement value   [ ]   _____

Contents value determined by:
    Guesstimate   [ ]   _____
    Personal inventory   [ ]   _____
    Average value per room   [ ]   _____

Contents of each room listed by:
    Videotape   [ ]   _____
    Inventory form   [ ]   _____
    Personal listing   [ ]   _____

HOMEOWNERS INSURANCE CHECKLIST

	Insured	Amount

4. Special Riders on Certain Properties

	Insured	Amount
Jewelry	[ ]	———
Furs	[ ]	———
Silverware	[ ]	———
Art	[ ]	———
Other Collectibles	[ ]	———

For more information,
see page 99.

HOMEOWNER'S INSURANCE COST COMPARISON WORKSHEET

COVERAGES	Ins. Co. No. 1	Limits	Ins. Co. No. 2	Limits
Home	_____	_____	_____	_____
Detached Structures	_____	_____	_____	_____
Contents	_____	_____	_____	_____
Special Items				
A. Jewelry	_____	_____	_____	_____
B. Furs	_____	_____	_____	_____
C. Silverware	_____	_____	_____	_____
D. Art	_____	_____	_____	_____
E. Other _____	_____	_____	_____	_____
Additional Living Expenses	_____	_____	_____	_____
Off-Premises Coverages	_____	_____	_____	_____
Liability	_____	_____	_____	_____
A. Voluntary Medical	_____	_____	_____	_____

HOMEOWNERS
INSURANCE
COST
COMPARISON
WORKSHEET
(Cont.)

	Ins. Co. No. 1	Limits	Ins. Co. No. 2	Limits
B. Voluntary Property Damage				
Other				
Property Deductible				

HOMEOWNERS INSURANCE COST COMPARISON WORKSHEET (Cont.)

	Ins. Co. No. 1 (Check if included)	Ins. Co. No. 2 (Check if included)
PERILS		
Fire, Lightning, Windstorm, or Hail	[ ]	[ ]
Explosion, Riot, Civil Commotion	[ ]	[ ]
Vandalism and Malicious Mischief	[ ]	[ ]
Theft or Smoke Damage	[ ]	[ ]
Falling Objects, Weight of Ice, Snow, or Sleet	[ ]	[ ]
Collapse of Buildings, Aircraft, Vehicles	[ ]	[ ]
Accidental Discharge, Leakage, or Overflow of Water or Steam Within Plumbing or Heating Appliance	[ ]	[ ]
Freezing of Plumbing, Heating, and Air Conditioning System	[ ]	[ ]
All Perils Except Flood, Earthquake, and Landslide	[ ]	[ ]

ANNUAL PREMIUM

Ins. Co. No. 1 _____ Annual Premium $ _____

Ins. Co. No. 2 _____ Annual Premium $ _____

For more information, see page 101.

PROPERTY LOSS REPORTING FORM

Name: _____

Address: _____

Telephone: _____

Date and Time of Loss: _____

Kind of Loss (Fire, Theft, Vandalism): _____

Location of Loss: _____

_____

Description of Loss: _____

_____

_____

_____

To Whom Reported: _____   *Telephone:* _____
(Police Department if a theft.)

Insurance Adjuster Assigned: _____   *Telephone:* _____

List of Damaged Items:

Item Description	Value	Proof of Value (appraisal, receipts, pictures, or video tape)
_____	_____	_____
_____	_____	_____
_____	_____	_____
_____	_____	_____
_____	_____	_____
_____	_____	_____

For more information, see page 101.

ACCIDENT REPORTING FORM

Name: _____

Address: _____

Telephone: _____

Date and Time: _____

Location: _____

To Whom Reported: _____ Telephone: _____
(Police Department or Insurance Agent)

Brief Description of Accident: _____

_____

Injured/Property Owner—Name: _____

Address: _____ Telephone: _____

Property Damaged: _____

_____

_____

_____

Witness
Name   Address   Telephone

_____

_____

Best time for your insurance company adjuster to contact you: ____

Telephone (if not same as above): _____

Insurance Adjuster assigned to claim and telephone:

_____

For more information,
see page 103.

AUTOMOBILE INSURANCE CHECKLIST

Coverages	Check If Covered
Bodily Injury	[ ]

Limits: Each Person _____ Each Occurrence _____

Property Damage Limits: _____	[ ]

Comprehensive Coverage	[ ]

Deductible _____

Collision Coverage	[ ]

Deductible _____

Car Rental _____	[ ]

Medical Coverage Limit _____	[ ]

Uninsured Motorists	[ ]

Limits: Each Person _____ Each Occurrence _____

Underinsured Motorists	[ ]

Limits: Each Person _____ Each Occurrence _____

Accidental Death and Dismemberment	[ ]

Limits _____

Stereo Unit, CB Radio, or Telephone	[ ]

Permanently Attached [ ]   Unattached [ ]

For more information,
see page 107.

INSURANCE PREMIUM COST COMPARISON

Coverages	Ins. Co. _____ Car No. 1	Car No. 2	Ins. Co. _____ Car No. 1	Car No. 2	Ins. Co. _____ Car No. 1	Car No. 2
Bodily Injury						
Limits of _____	$	$	$	$	$	$
Property Damage						
Limits of _____						
Comprehensive						
Deductible _____						
Collision						
Deductible _____						
Medical Payments						
Limit _____						
Uninsured Motorist						
Limit _____						
Underinsured Motorist						
Limits of _____						

INSURANCE PREMIUM COST COMPARISON

Coverages	Ins. Co. Car No. 1	Car No. 2	Ins. Co. Car No. 1	Car No. 2	Ins. Co. Car No. 1	Car No. 2
Accidental Death and Dismemberment						
Limits of _____						
Special Equipment Covered						
TOTAL	$ ____	$ ____	$ ____	$ ____	$ ____	$ ____

For more information, see page 107.

AUTOMOBILE ACCIDENT REPORTING FORM

(Keep in Car)

Accident Information

Date: _____ Time: _____

Location: _____
(Be as precise as possible)

_____

_____

Brief Description of Accident: _____

_____

_____

_____

_____

Other Cars Involved

Driver's Name: _____

Address: _____

Telephone: (____) _____

Driver's License: _____ State: _____

Auto Make: _____ Year: _____ Type: _____ Color: _____

Registration Number: _____ State: _____

Owner of Auto: _____

Address: _____

Telephone: (____) _____

Insurance Company or Agency: _____

_____

AUTOMOBILE ACCIDENT REPORTING FORM

Driver's Name: _____

Address: _____

Telephone: (_____) _____

Driver's License: _____ State: _____

Auto Make: _____ Year: _____ Type: _____ Color: _____

Registration Number: _____ State: _____

Owner of Auto: _____

Address: _____

Telephone: (_____) _____

Insurance Company or Agency: _____

_____

Passengers or Other Persons Injured

Name: _____ Address: _____

_____

Name: _____ Address: _____

_____

Name: _____ Address: _____

_____

Property Damage Other Than to Cars

Description: _____

_____

_____

AUTOMOBILE ACCIDENT REPORTING FORM

Witnesses and/or Passengers

Name　　　　　*Address*　　　　　*Telephone*

_____

_____

_____

_____

Police Who Took Report

Name: _____　*Report No.:* _____

Diagram of Accident

For more information,
see page 107.

TRANSITION PLAN CHECKLIST
At Once

		Completed
1.	Make funeral arrangements	[ ]
2.	Decide on obituary notices	[ ]
3.	Notify relatives	[ ]
4.	Notify friends	[ ]
5.	Open a new checking account in your name	[ ]

Within the First 30 Days

		Completed
1.	Get 20 certified copies of the death certificate	[ ]
2.	Put all joint checking and savings accounts in your name	[ ]
3.	Establish an "estate" bank account	[ ]
4.	Notify all insurance companies involved and file claims	[ ]
5.	Review the auto insurance for accidental death, medical, or other coverages	[ ]
6.	Check the medical policies for any time limitations for filing claims and for additional coverages	[ ]
7.	Check for travel accident coverage	[ ]
8.	Report death to Social Security	[ ]
9.	Apply for Social Security benefits	[ ]
10.	Report death to Veteran's Administration and apply for benefits	[ ]
11.	Notify husband's employers or associates to file for benefits	[ ]
12.	Check on Workers Compensation benefits	[ ]
13.	Check husband's possible life insurance coverage with clubs, associations, credit cards, or other organizations	[ ]

TRANSITION PLAN CHECKLIST (Cont.)

Completed

14. *Have securities transferred to your name* [ ]

15. *Have U.S. Savings Bonds placed in your name* [ ]

16. *Open a safe-deposit box in your name* [ ]

17. *Notify IRA and Keogh accounts* [ ]

18. *Review Chapter 5, Borrowing* [ ]

19. *Review income tax records* [ ]

20. *Other* _____ [ ]

21. *Other* _____ [ ]

22. *Other* _____ [ ]

23. *Other* _____ [ ]

24. *Other* _____ [ ]

25. *Other* _____ [ ]

TRANSITION PLAN CHECKLIST (Cont.)

Within the Next 60 Days

Completed

1. *Select an attorney to represent your interest and to file husband's will* [ ]

2. *Pick an accountant for financial affairs and for filing estate and inheritance tax returns* [ ]

3. *Transfer real estate title to your name* [ ]

4. *Transfer title on cars to your name* [ ]

Completed

5. Change name on auto and homeowner's insurance policies   [   ]

6. Cancel or change all credit or charge cards to your name   [   ]

7. Change name under which utilities are billed   [   ]

8. Change listing in the telephone directory   [   ]

9. Review the beneficiaries on your life insurance policies   [   ]

10. Review your own medical insurance   [   ]

11. Revise your will   [   ]

12. Notify creditors of your situation   [   ]

13. Select a financial advisor   [   ]

14. Other _____   [   ]

15. Other _____   [   ]

TRANSITION PLAN CHECKLIST (Cont.)

Within the Next 6 Months

Completed

1. *Complete a new budget* [ ]

2. *Review your life insurance needs* [ ]

3. *Update your will* [ ]

4. *Review all worksheets in the book* [ ]

5. *Review your disability plan* [ ]

6. *Review your investment plan* [ ]

7. *Review old records of checks and bank statements* [ ]

8. *Monitor the executor* [ ]

For more information, see page 112.

CHECKLIST OF EXECUTOR'S DUTIES

Completed

1. *File an annual report with the court showing property received* [ ]

2. *File an annual report showing amount spent from estate* [ ]

3. *File an inventory with the court on all money and property received (normally three months after appointed)* [ ]

4. *Secure reimbursement for all costs paid to the courts by you* [ ]

5. *Avoid any individual financial transactions with the estate* [ ]

6. *Open a bank account in the name of the estate* [ ]

7. *Set up a separate account for each ward of the estate* [ ]

8. *Obtain court permission to spend estate's money* [ ]

9. *Obtain court permission to sell, lease, or invest property of the estate* [ ]

10. *Have the value of the property of the estate appraised* [ ]

11. *Deal with creditors* [ ]

For more information, see page 116.

JOB-SKILLS WORKSHEET

Work I'd Love

_____

_____

_____

_____

_____

_____

_____

_____

_____

_____

_____

_____

_____

_____

_____

_____

_____

_____

_____

My Skills and Accomplishments

_____

_____

_____

_____

_____

_____

_____

_____

_____

_____

_____

_____

_____

_____

_____

_____

_____

_____

_____

For more information,
see page 122.

FORMAL NETWORKING RECORD

Name	Organization/Company	Address and Telephone	Results

For more information, see page 124.

CASUAL NETWORKING RECORD

Name and Company	Date and Place of Contact	Person to Contact	Results

For more information, see text page 124.

RÉSUMÉ WORKSHEET

Address: _____   Telephone: _____

_____   Messages: _____

Career Accomplishments
(In order of importance)

1. _____

2. _____

3. _____

4. _____

5. _____

Education
(List highest education achievement first)

Honors or Activities: _____

_____

Special Courses: _____

_____

Work History
(Starting with most recent)

1. _____

2. _____

3. _____

4. _____

References

1. _____

2. _____

3. _____

For more information,
see page 127.

RÉSUMÉ TRACKING SHEET

Résumé Sent to	Telephone	Person to Contact	First Call Date	Remarks

For more information, see page 128.

1. *What are your strengths?*

_____

2. *What are your weaknesses?*

_____

3. *Why do you want this position?*

_____

4. *Why are you interested in this company?*

_____

5. *Tell me a little bit about yourself.*

_____

6. *Why haven't you worked for so long?*

_____

7. *What did you think of your previous employer?*

_____

8. *What do you expect to do in five years?*

_____

9. *Are you planning on additional education?*

_____

10. *What salary do you want?*

_____

11. *Which of your past jobs have you liked the best?*

_____

12. *Why did you leave your last job?*

_____

LIKELY INTERVIEW QUESTIONS

13. *Why haven't you got a job yet?*

   _____

14. *Which of your past jobs have you liked the least?*

   _____

15. *Tell me about your best manager in the past.*

   _____

16. *What kind of people do you work best with?*

   _____

17. *What kind of people do you have the most difficulty in dealing with?*

   _____

18. *How far would you like to go in the company?*

   _____

19. *Why should we hire you?*

   _____

20. *How long do you plan on staying with us?*

   _____

21. *Can you work under pressure?*

   _____

22. *Have you hired or fired people before?*

   _____

23. *Are you willing to travel?*

   _____

24. *Are you willing to relocate?*

   _____

25. *Do you like to be creative?*

   _____

26. *How would you describe your personality?*

   _____

27. *May we contact your present employer?*

   _____

28. *May we contact your references?*

   _____

29. *Are you considering any other job?*

   _____

For more information,
see page 128.

RESEARCHING PROSPECTIVE EMPLOYERS

1. *What is their business?*

   _____

2. *How long have they been in this business?*

   _____

3. *What is the goal of the organization?*

   _____

4. *Who is their largest competitor?*

   _____

5. *How are they doing this year?*

   _____

6. *What type of employees are they looking for?*

   _____

7. *How many employees do they have?*

   _____

8. *Why is this position open?*

   _____

9. *Who had this position before?*

   _____

10. *Where is this person now?*

    _____

11. *What are the promotion possibilities?*

    _____

12. *To whom would you be reporting?*

    _____

For more information, see page 129.